RELIGIOUS LIFE AS ADVENTURE

RELIGIOUS LIFE AS ADVENTURE

Renewal, Refounding, or Reform?

Rev. Albert Di Ianni, SM

ALBA·HOUSE   NEW·YORK

SOCIETY OF ST. PAUL, 2187 VICTORY BLVD., STATEN ISLAND, NEW YORK 10314

Library of Congress Cataloging-in-Publication Data

DiIanni, Albert.
    Religious life as adventure: renewal, refounding, or reform? /
Albert DiIanni.
        p.   cm.
    Includes bibliographical references.
    ISBN 0-8189-0716-9
    BX2385.D55   1994
    255 — dc20   94-30399
                                                  CIP

Produced and designed in the United States of America by the
Fathers and Brothers of the Society of St. Paul,
2187 Victory Boulevard, Staten Island, New York 10314,
as part of their communications apostolate.

ISBN: 0-8189-0716-9

Printing Information:

Current Printing - first digit	1	2	3	4	5	6	7	8	9	10

Year of Current Printing - first year shown

1994	1995	1996	1997	1998	1999

*Dedicated to
my mother and
to the memory of my father*

TABLE OF CONTENTS

INTRODUCTION

A member of my religious community, a close friend and a poet by nature, once remarked that we would not see an increase in religious vocations until religious life was once again experienced as a spiritual adventure. We must once again be swept up in a dream, spurred by a vision and a quest, listen to a message spoken in the deep reaches of our heart. This alone will revive the fearlessness, the will to commit ourselves for life and never look back. The experience of religious life is flattened into bourgeois dullness when it conforms to the utilitarian instincts of a world bent on maximizing lowest common denominator desires. It will fail to excite because it is too stuck to the earth. It is my hope, by means of this book, to rekindle the wonder and the poetry, to help religious life regain its divine attraction as a special form of love for Christ and for those He desires to save.

The renewal of the consecrated life that has been in progress since Vatican II has cultural and political aspects as well as religious ones. Politically, a reader of Tocqueville's *Democracy in America* might interpret it as a move from aristocracy to democracy. American religious life has deep roots in Europe and in its trip across the Atlantic it preserved elements of a European-style aristocracy. While religious men of an earlier day did minister diligently among the poor of an immigrant Church, their training also taught them to remain aloof from the world, and to indulge in a kind of spiritual preening in the pursuit of perfection. Spirituality could at times take the form of great introspection and of a tending to "the beautiful soul."

On the other hand, even aristocratic culture has desirable features, like a sense of self-worth, dignity, grace, and a striving for excellence. In fact, if we who are members of religious congregations scan our lives, most will find that we were attracted to the religious life by some spiritual aristocrat, a "beautiful" person in our family, neighborhood or congregation, who spoke to us in accents of wisdom and holiness and was a symbol of God's presence. What impresses us most about people is not what they do, but who they are.

Vatican II challenged religious congregations to divest themselves of many accouterments of a fading European culture while reclaiming and deepening the charism of their founders. As a part of its effort to find a proper this-worldly role for Christianity, *Perfectae Caritatis* and subsequent legislation urged religious to re-read their founding charism in light of the needs of the times and to eliminate outdated structures. Realizing that the Church was on the brink of burgeoning into a world-Church, the Council spurred the whole Church away from a classical to a historical mode of consciousness.

Propelled by Vatican II and influenced by the cultural revolution of the 1960's and 1970's, American religious congregations introduced many startling developments. The lives of founders were mined, charisms were researched, new constitutions written, and new criteria developed for selecting and retaining apostolates. In choosing apostolates, strict product orientation — delivering education or health services — gave way to a market orientation in which a congregation assessed the social needs of the times and tailored ministries to fit priorities or "consumer" demand. Self-enclosed, traditional congregations urged their leaders to collaborate with other congregations through recently founded conferences of major superiors. Dialogue and concern for individual development replaced the commands of a strict obedience in formation programs and in the process of assigning of religious to various ministries. Structures and models of government were modified to incorporate principles of subsidiarity and collegiality in decision-making. The boundaries between consecrated and lay life were blurred by the acceptance of lay associates and by the enlisting of a number of lay volunteers into the missionary endeavor. The contemplative dimension of religious life was often deemphasized in favor of a so-called prophetic dimension, interpreted as a dedication to the poor and to causes of peace and justice.

So dramatic were these changes that at times religious congregations seemed to be discarding golden grains along with the husks. A whole religious sub-culture was dismantled and a long-standing vision of religious life came under question. The very project of religious life as an ecclesial reality valid for our day was placed in doubt. The setting aside of the religious habit was the most evident change, but more drastic was the whole revision of obedience, government structures and the practices of common life and prayer. In many female congregations the role of the local superior was completely discarded, most matters were decided by consensus and in the area of apostolic appointment great scope was given to personal desires and fulfillment. Corporate apostolates in education and health care were increasingly abandoned and replaced by individual apostolates or ministries conducted by smaller groups.

It cannot be denied that, from a psychological point of view, many of the changes were salutary. Minute rules and regulations that stifled growth and engendered pettiness were removed. Responsible adulthood rather than childlikeness became the goal of religious formation. Scrupulosity tended to disappear. Individuals were encouraged to develop their talents and creativity, and express their desires and opinions. Apostolic choices were more diverse, adapted to a person's talents and legitimate desires, and often responded more adequately to real needs of the times. A life of prayer that often seemed mechanical and based on rote recitation became freer and more personal, preached retreats were replaced by directed retreats, and many found strength and solace in a renewed form of the Ignatian Exercises.

Despite these and other positive results, a sense of a corporate identity and purpose seemed to have been lost, the image of a group called together by the Lord and living a regular life of mutual edification that helped them grow in holiness while attending to the needs of others. Some critics complained that, along with particular devotions, devotion itself was disappearing from many religious houses, and that for some religious the literal following of Christ no longer seemed a primary aim. Others believed that in the post-Vatican II period the pursuit of American-style pluralism had become an end in itself, with the resultant loss of common purpose. Hearts seemed divided. In their life and appearance many female religious seemed indistinguishable from secular social workers. Writings about religious life were heavily laden with the jargon of sociology and business management and less redolent of the Gospel. Gone was the lively sense of "vocation," of having been called by God to a religious adventure. Partly because of this, vocations in the first world dried up, many professed religious left the ranks, and of those who remained, a good number lived on the periphery of their community and maintained only perfunctory relations with the group.

In spite of all this, members of the male and female conferences of major superiors — CMSM and LCWR — persisted in heaping praise upon the changes and continued to devise a plethora of meetings and workshops. Most commentators on religious life preferred to stress the beneficial features of the new freedoms and seemed oblivious of the chaotic aspects of the renewal. But recently a number of writers have begun to ask whether the renewal itself had not foundered. Some questioned whether it had not yielded to faddism and at times yoked itself uncritically to the current ideology of political correctness. Others complained that, despite the veneer of a participative democracy, the bureaucracies that replaced "mother superior" had found more effective ways of suppressing dissent and exercising control over the group. New calls arose for a mid-course correction in the process of renewal. Most of these calls were similar in being critiques of the so-called "liberal model" of renewal in vogue since Vatican II. They differed, however, in their positive recommendations, some urging a deeper probing of the great spiritualities and charisms of our founders,[1] and others endorsing a move from liberalism to an even more radical pluralism.[2]

The compilers of a major sociological study (Nygren and Ukeritis) have surfaced several major problems in contemporary religious life. One is the lack of sufficient role-clarity especially among female religious and younger members of both male and female congregations. Another is the dichotomy which often exists between a congregation's expressed commitments and its actual behavior. The study shows that many members of groups that have made a preferential option for the poor in their mission statements are often reluctant to leave traditional ministries among the comfortable. A third major problem revolved around the area of leadership. The study signals the dearth of effective leaders capable of articulating a vision for the future which is also bolstered by concrete strategies. It also questions the validity of the wholesale and uncritical introduction of secular democratic structures into religious life. If earlier authority structures were too rigid, current processes of consensus often end up in bland compromises, while processes based on personal discernment encourage participants to interpret personal wishes as movements of the Holy Spirit. A major conclusion of the Nygren-Ukeritis study is that no religious group seems to attract a substantial number of new members unless it has strong leadership, makes strong demands on its members, and has visible rituals and

[1] Cf. Elizabeth McDonough, "Beyond the Liberal Model: Quo Vadis," *Review for Religious*, March/April, 1991.

[2] Cf. Mary Jo Leddy, *Reweaving Religious Life: Beyond the Liberal Model*, Mystic, Conn., Twenty-Third Publications, 1990.

practices differentiating itself from other groups.

Where do we go from here? It is clear that we cannot beat a fundamentalist retreat to the past. Vatican II and its call for *aggiornamento* cannot be rejected. On the contrary, we must enter more deeply into the Council and plumb its true spirit. We must recognize that it called not only for updating and change, but for a greater depth of spirituality. If religious were asked to discard mere formalisms it was in order to accomplish a profound rediscovery of their charism and thus become a more powerful spiritual force in the Church and world. Religious were to be for the Church what the Church should be for the world. The principal question we must ask at this point is: "Are we where Vatican II wanted us to be when it invited us to change?" As compared with thirty years ago, is religious life as it is lived today a better expression of the charism of the founder and a more vivid symbol of the core of the Gospel for the Church and the world?

The answer to this question is not evident. What is clear to the shallowest observer is that the renewal of religious life cannot consist solely in absorbing uncritically every element of contemporary American culture. Inculturation of the Gospel and of religious life in different cultures is important, but inculturation is a complex sifting process. Since each culture has negative as well as positive aspects, it is important that in inculturating we take both into consideration. We must strive to modify religious life in view of those elements in our culture which are in conformity with the Gospel, and these elements are significant. On the other hand, we must also develop new ascetic features for religious life to help us counteract those aspects of the culture which are corrosive and serve to impinge upon a life lived in full harmony with the mysteries of the Gospel.

American society has enviable qualities admired by foreigners. Immigrants to the United States are startled by the extent of our religious and political freedoms, by the relative peace among great pluralism, by our ability to participate in the political process not only by voting but by demonstrating for civil rights, criticizing political leaders and speaking out in various ways. These rights are precious and must never be taken for granted. On the other hand, we must also recognize serious deficiencies of our society, decadent elements that bespeak decline. These elements show up most dramatically in MTV with its glorification of a hedonistic individualism in which personal desires become paramount, an MTV riddled with pornographic sex, violence, satanism and blasphemy. They are manifest, too, in the explosion of random homicide, teenage pregnancy, divorce, casual adultery, abortion-on-demand, adolescent suicide, and in the general decline of the family, all recently documented in a Carnegie Corporation report on the needs of children. Reflecting on the divorce statistics in this study, one author concludes that "the naive suppositions of liberals in the 1970's — that women could afford to go it alone, that family disruption would cause no lasting harm to children, that the two-parent family need not be the norm — have all proved spurious."[3] American childhood is no longer a time of innocence and joy. Public schools in our cities are often places of terror where some young people carry guns and others require counselling and meditation-rooms to cope with the murder of a friend. When we hear young people say — as I have — that they would like to be shot in order to experience a sense of importance, clearly something has gone wrong.

The cultural move toward crime, violence and casual sex is not unrelated to an underlying philosophy of arbitrary freedom that leads to one-parent families and resists imposing discipline on children for fear of damaging youthful self-esteem. Has our democracy not become excessively permissive and egalitarian? Has not tolerance become so overriding a moral duty that it has leached out other important values, values essential to morality and family? Does not a tolerance without limits actually destroy the social structures that make a life of freedom and dignity possible? It is becoming clearer and clearer, for example,

[3] Cf. "Broken Homes, Broken Lives," *America*, May 14, 1994, p. 3.

that illegitimacy is a major factor in creating crime, drug abuse and welfare crises. Have we not also yielded to a philosophy that blames all social sins on economic inequalities and in the process erodes a sense of personal responsibility? And, more relevantly, how far have some of these attitudes shaped the contemporary renewal of religious life?

In our admirable effort to exercise a preferential option for the poor in both the first and third worlds, have we not neglected an equally important challenge, the conversion and evangelization of an increasingly paganized mainstream America? In this line, has not the retreat of Jesuits and members of other religious congregations from the education apostolate been the loss of a golden opportunity to bring the challenge of the Gospel squarely before our culture and its leadership? Must we not turn our apostolic efforts to a critical evaluation of an American culture too reliant on science as the sole vehicle to truth and a value-system too bent upon the release of instincts?

It is important that criticisms of the form that the renewal of religious life has taken since Vatican II not be dismissed as mere stirrings of a romantic nostalgia regarding the past. The following essays share their conviction that the renewal of religious life cannot simply continue as it is. Five of them were previously published as articles in reviews and are re-published here in lengthened and modified form. In the order of appearance, they are: "Religious Life and Religion," *Review for Religious*, July-August 1992, vol. 51, pp. 527-539; "Religious Life and Modernity," *Review for Religious*, May/June 1991, vol. 50, pp. 339-351; "Vocations and the Laicization of Religious Life," *America*, March 14, 1987, pp. 207-211; "Faith and Justice: A Delicate Balance," *America*, July 15-22, 1989, pp. 32-36 and 45; and "Religious Vocations: New Signs of the Times," *Review for Religious*, September/October 1993, vol. 52, pp. 745-763. I thank the editors of both *America* and the *Review for Religious* for granting permission to reprint these articles. These essays examine the impact of modern culture on different aspects of religious life, on formation, vocations, efforts in social justice, and on its very faith. Added are three new essays on celibate chastity, community life, and the need for vision in religious leadership. In all of them I insist that the ongoing renewal of religious life be based on new assumptions and on an inventive retrieval of a lost adventure and lost faith. This will not be accomplished by attitudinal surveys alone, no matter how competent. Rather, in prayer and reflection, we must ask fresh questions, break new ground, devise other metaphors.

Are we where God intended us to be when Vatican II invited us to change? I believe we are not. In our rush to de-structure religious life and fly from oppressive aspects of our institutions, we failed to realize that above all else, our founders were builders of institutions. They were entrepreneurs who launched forth to build up a *corps* of mutual conversion for the work of the Lord, a body of mutual edification that would give flesh in the world to a particular aspect of the Gospel. It was precisely because they founded institutions, ways of life, that they were able to gather people to selflessly dedicate their entire being. They were not poets flush with metaphor, nor theologians spinning a system, nor solely saints living a personal holy life; they were and are what we call them — founders. Theologians are believed, poets are read, but founders are followed.

One implication of this is that a founder's charism cannot be understood independently from the institution he or she founded. The charism of the foundations is not a mere set of ideas, a free-floating ethos that each person is free to live out in his or her own way. Abstracted from its corporate and structural aspect, the charism's meaning is partly lost. In fact, the original rules and structures may be a privileged locus to study its meaning.

An example might be helpful. The major historian of a male religious congregation founded in the 19th century made a study of those directives of the congregation's founder which seemed most to jar contemporary attitudes. An instance of these was the founder's policy that on a monthly basis each member of the community should go to the local superior, kneel before him, confess his faults, open his heart to him, and request his counsel. The historian's motive was in no way to urge a literal return to this practice, but to reveal an important aspect of the founder's concept of a superior, that he not be primarily an efficient administrator, but a true spiritual leader, vitally and concretely concerned about the spiritual life and development of each member of the community. The founder's insistence that the community member kneel before the superior had nothing to do with feudal hierarchical practices. The kneeling was intended, rather, to cause embarrassment to the superior and to set a tone of mutual humility in the hope that all power-plays be set aside and that person might meet person authentically before God. At the end of his analysis the historian urges that with or without kneeling, and possibly less frequently than every month, superiors and individual community members should once again meet in faith-filled dialogue. In his opinion, the updating of common practices must not fail to express the spiritual realities upon which the congregation is founded and without which it has no right to exist.

Passion will not return to religious life nor will young people join until congregations retrieve the sense of a *corporate* and *religious* adventure that impelled our founders to sacrifice and heroism. Reflecting on the yearnings of the young, Paul Claudel said that more than pleasure they desire heroism. This seemed borne out in the huge youth rallies with Pope John Paul II in 1993 in Denver, Colorado. It is time to reclaim the art of lifelong commitment to a group and through it to challenge the young to come to the aid of the Church at a time of crisis. This will be achieved by moving beyond concepts of sociology and business management, to a stage in the renewal that is at once a veritable *reform* seeking its inspiration at the city walls of Avila and in the mystical accents of *The Ascent of Mount Carmel*. A lifestyle that is bourgeois, a religious life that has been content with a superficial *aggiornamento* and is too eager to incorporate the values of the society that surrounds it, no longer raises questions and cannot exercise a critical function.

1. RELIGIOUS LIFE AND RELIGION

A critique of current attempts at renewing religious life
must deal with fundamental questions before it moves on
to specific aspects of religious life. This was brought home
to me during my participation in recent discussions on the
"refounding" of religious life. They turned out to be quite
passionate and at times ended in discord. Admittedly the
groups involved were tired and overworked, but this was
not the whole explanation. The heat so manifest in
exchanges about potential cures for the ills of
contemporary religious life springs from a deeper source,
from a basic disagreement about the nature of Christianity
and of religion.

When I first encountered the notion of "refounding"
currently in vogue, I welcomed it as an improvement over
"renewal" because it seemed to demand a deeper
conversion and a more radical rebuilding. It brought to
mind the Carmelite reform at the hands of Teresa and John
of the Cross through an inventive retrieval of the pristine
spirit and discipline of the founders. Refounding seemed to
invite us to create new structures, new symbolic
expressions of the very being of our congregations, in order
to better launch forth upon a religious journey demanding
great sacrifice and an engagement with the world that
remained in some way separate from the world.

Resistance to the notion of refounding mounted in
me, however, with the repeated calls to identify "change-
agents" in the group whose principal aim was to foster
creativity in ministry or to develop alternative community
lifestyles. The more speakers limited their discussions to

talk about "delivery systems" for change, paraded leadership models derived from anthropology or introduced yet another corporate reflection technique borrowed from business psychology — the more they discussed only *means* — the more I felt I was being bundled down some primrose path. Before I discuss means I want to discuss *goals*, before I accept help to move forward, I want to determine where I, where we, should want to go. This is possibly because I suspect that I do not want to go where certain speakers want to lead me, or that a speaker's advice about means carries some hidden freight about goals with which I do not concur.

In a very recent conversation about refounding, I suddenly found myself compelled to ask the interlocutors some strange, basic questions, not about religious life but about religion: "What, for you, constitutes the heart of the Christian religion?" I asked the group. "What is its basic meaning or purpose? What engenders religion in the first place?" Such questions came to mind because I suddenly realized that our disagreement lay at a deep level, that we could not simply assume we would all answer such fundamental questions in the same way. This was not because anyone had expressly denied any belief that I held, but because some seemed to deflect or sidestep certain questions as old-fashioned or as not in line with the particular action-steps being recommended.

The urge to ask fundamental questions comes upon me especially when I sense that religion is being reduced to sociology, psychology, or even to morality, be it personal, social, or ecological morality. In fact, the temptation to reduce religion to morality fires me up more than the grosser sociological or psychological reductions, because it is more subtle and plausible, and thus more seductive.

But let me put my own cards on the table. What do I believe is at the heart of the Christian religion? (I will ignore the esoteric distinction drawn by some between faith and religion and the theory that Christianity is not a religion but a faith.) Though Christianity like other religions is an amalgam of many components, I believe that its strictly religious aspect lies in its being an answer to the experience of human contingency and the contingency of the world. Most people at some time in their lives have felt wonder that the world exists at all and have faced into the void of their own death. They moved beyond the taken-for-grantedness of the world and become frightened by the thought that nothing at all might have existed and no possibility of anything. They have wondered if life has an ultimate meaning or if humans were but a sport of nature. Christianity's central doctrine is that the world need not have existed and that it was the object of creation by a good God. A Christian believer is convinced that at the center of the universe is not a surd but a personal Love.

The philosopher Ludwig Wittgenstein was not a believer. Norman Malcolm, his former student and biographer, says that he could not be called a religious person, but that he was passionately interested in religion and always seemed close to the *possibility* of religion. Wittgenstein once produced two examples of what he considered *bonafide* religious experiences as opposed to moral or aesthetic ones. He respected them even if he thought that in entertaining them he was running up against the limits of language. One was the experience of uncanniness that the world exists at all. The second was the conviction he had at times that whatever might happen, he would be safe.

Neither of these experiences point of necessity to the existence of a transcendent God. But they provide the experiential ground, the feeling base, the springboard from which many people move to affirm the existence of God. It is in such feelings and experiences that the affirmation that God exists is existentially grounded, becomes more than an intellectual proposition, takes root, finds a home. The first experience is the sense that a fleeting world must be rooted in a stable fundamental Reality. The second bespeaks a trust that cannot be explained without the presence of a loving center of the universe.

My own thoughts about religion revolve about experiences of this type. Admittedly my idea of religion has strong mystical overtones; it is our response to radical contingency and in its most primitive and deepest meaning has little to do with morality. Religion refers primarily to a "holy" space out of which we and the world spring and gives rise to the imperative for each of us to become holy, to live our life in and for God.

Beyond this, I know that religion and morality are intimately intertwined and that a religious or holy person must also be morally good. One can hardly be holy and evil. Holiness means, in part, being extraordinarily kind, socially just, honest, temperate, a peacemaker. Yet it cannot be reduced to the practice of these moral virtues. For it is conceivable that someone could be morally good, could follow punctiliously the rules of a moral system, foster social justice, be chaste or kind, and yet not be a religious person. He or she could be moral out of personal taste, temperament, for aesthetic reasons, or out of natural sympathy toward others, and not because of his or her relationship to God. Philippa Foot, an Oxford moral philosopher and avowed atheist, once told a seminar group that she was such a moral person, and that she refused to be patronized by being called an "anonymous Christian."

A Christian religious person not only acts morally but also sees the world in a new way — that it is dependent for its very existence on a transcendent reality, and that this makes all the difference. Because it is focused upon the transcendent, the Christian vision has specific ethical implications different from Enlightenment theories which place the human person or freedom at the center of the moral endeavor. For the Christian the primary response to the world is not that of owner and Promethean creator but of humble and obedient creature, not an entrepreneurial relishing of power and freedom but a Marian gratitude before God for all that God has wrought. Out of this Christian gratitude is born the imperative to love God and reverence God's creation, the willingness to allow God to express the divine mercy through us, especially toward the weak and the abandoned. This Christian gratitude and its ethical implications are nourished and deepened through a close union with God in prayer.

It is this fundamental vision, it seems to me, which should be at the heart of the life of every consecrated religious. If they are to be prophetic, it is in this: that in their lives they point constantly to the transcendent moment of the universe and try to develop what it means. It is up to each religious congregation to decide how it will express this, but it is essential. As a Christian I am impressed both when I see priests, sisters or brothers wrapped in contemplation of God and when I see them picking up a dying person from the streets. When I see one of them unremittingly engaged in both, I believe I am in the presence of a saint.

Some contemporary Catholics as well as members of religious congregations seem to have lost sight of the transcendent pole of Christianity. Their model of Christianity has become what Charles Davis labels *pragmatic.* The pragmatic version of Christianity arose, he says, when "the Christian religion ceased to function mythically as an overarching totality. . . . The emphasis therefore shifted to Christianity as a practical way of life or ethical system. This is still conceived in religious terms, such as the fatherhood of God and the brotherhood of God's children, the kingdom of righteousness. . . . But all these expressions are different ways of formulating the moral imperatives governing human existence."[1]

Both conservatives and liberals have to some degree made this pragmatic shift in Christianity. Conservatives stress personal and family morality, and such questions as abortion and euthanasia, while progressives talk incessantly about social justice, ecology and feminist rights. Future historians may judge that the Vatican itself, but to a lesser degree, has been drawn into what I am characterizing as an over-emphasis on morality. They may well remember Pope John Paul II as the "morality Pope,"

[1] *What is Living, What is Dead in Christianity Today?* San Francisco, Harper and Row, 1986, p. 39.

because of his repeated statements about both personal as well as social morality. In practice, if not in theory, love of neighbor and enemy seem to have taken precedence over concern about union with God. Today's heresies all seem to be moral heresies. Not many Catholics seem overly concerned about dogmas, about trinitarian, soteriological or Christological errors. And yet the history of the early Church reveals that this was not always so. (Should we not fashion a brand-new trinitarian heresy to spur more thought about God and less about ourselves!) In this excessive emphasis on morality the modern Church reflects the tenor of our secularized times, the age that mistook the world for God.

In the late 1960's, a time noted for its air of revolution, our seminary faculty once gathered the seminarians for a discussion on the question: "What are the most important qualities for being a priest and religious today?" Some suggested approachability, others learning and competence, still others kindness or some other human virtue. I was surprised that no one spoke of holiness — a sure candidate just ten years before — and I pointed this out to the group. One of the seminarians fixed me with a stare and said with an air of disdain: "Just be human, Father!"

A few years ago, I had the pleasure of interviewing Kiko Argüello, the Spanish layman and artist who founded the Neo-Catechumenate movement, which offers a series of steps, a way, for modern Catholics to rediscover their baptism and be committed to evangelization. I played the devil's advocate and asked whether his way (*camino*) of training lay people over a period of years, did not produce an arrogant elite and end up creating more division than unity in parishes. His answer was in strict contrast to the seminarian's. He insisted that becoming a Christian today was not easy, as many priests trained since Vatican II seemed to believe. It did not suffice to simply shout the love-slogan. Belief that God exists and that Jesus is in some way the son of God is difficult in a secularized culture.

6

Beyond this our world of drugs and violence, suburban adultery and abortion, euthanasia and consumerism, was full of snares. It would not be sufficient to simply limit our preaching to a form of positive reinforcement. People had to be called to a public confession of their belief in God Jesus, be led to a felt-need for conversion, be tested in their resolve, be supported by a tightly-knit community and be enriched through a warm and participative liturgy. Needed, in his view, was a method, a way, a structure, a catechumenate, to bring people squarely before their Baptism and its implications for their lives. In so many words he was saying that it was simplistic for the 1968 seminarian to have said: "Just be human, Father."

Yes, Christ is at work in the world wherever human good is being done, and we have to recognize and foster such work wherever we find it. We must also be aware, however, that to be a Catholic Christian it does not suffice to foster humanistic values. Besides demanding that we be moral root and branch, Catholicism demands belief in many strange things, like the Incarnation, the need for redemption, the Resurrection, the real presence of Jesus in the Eucharist, the role of Mary, and the like. As James Hitchcock has insisted, the idea of dogma is essential to Catholicism and dogma is important precisely because it protects us from the "almost fanatical drive which each epoch manifests to re-mold all of reality to suit its own specifications."[2]

For a time in my adolescence I wished I had been brought up neutral vis-a-vis religion, so that at the age of 21 I might consider all the major religions and choose among them without the prejudice of early Catholic training or brainwashing. But I know now that this is naive, for I have recognized that young people who have not been brought up in any religion end up by having no religious sentiment or religiosity. They tend to remain religion-neutral and are often unable to make a choice in favor of any religion. George Lindbeck, a Protestant theologian, believes that unless some religion is taught to

[2] "Eternity's Abiding Presence," in *Why Catholic?*, ed. John J. Delaney, N.Y., Image Books, 1980, p. 80.

us when we are young, unless we are brought up in some religious practices, we might not even be capable of religious experience. This may be exaggerated, but I am sure it contains a grain of truth. One thing is certain: No one is ever brought up in a vacuum of vision and values. If they do not absorb religious vision and values they will absorb the secular vision and a-religious values of the movies and television.

Especially in Europe several new lay Christian movements and religious orders have been born in full awareness of this — the Focolare movement, the San Egidio community, the neo-catechumenate, the Lion of Juda, etc. They all believe that becoming Christian in a secularized world is especially difficult. Secularization can be a purification of our faith and in many ways should be welcomed, but it contains its particular dangers. To navigate our way, they believe we need a method, a belonging to a new kind of Christian sub-culture provided by the new Christian movements and communities, all of which have their own form of *kenosis*, of abandoning and emptying oneself in preparation for a radical decision for Christ and God. Karl Rahner once declared: "A Christian in today's world will be a mystic or else he will not exist." And he went on to speak of mystagogy, the need to develop methods to lead people to see everything in God.

I believe that one reason why religious congregations are in a mere survival situation today is because in their admirable effort to take a positive view of the world they have identified religion too strongly with a humanistic morality that tends to be secularistic, individualistic and overly egalitarian in its emphases. History shows that almost all religious congregations enjoyed strong growth at their beginnings. They were exciting and attractive in part because they were new. But their major attraction lay elsewhere: the early members had a sense of a religious adventure and of a cause larger than themselves which rendered them willing to forego many personal rights and privileges. They were members of what has been called

³ Cf. Patricia
Wittberg, SC,
*Creating a Future
for Religious Life*,
New York,
Paulist Press,
1991, chapters 2,
3 and 4. See also
the use made of
these categories
by Elizabeth
McDonough, OP,
in "The Past is
Prologue: Quid
Agis?" in *Review
for Religious*, vol.
51, n. 1, Jan/Feb,
1992, pp. 78-99.

"intentional" communities as opposed to "associational" and "bureaucratic" ones" that have come into existence since Vatican II.³ They were quite unconcerned with self-expression and equality, and voluntarily surrendered some control over their choices not because they were naive and subservient (today's caricature), but because they were caught up in a higher religious cause and desired to forge themselves into a dynamic force for the Church and for God.

Most religious congregations were founded for three main purposes: (1) the salvation of the souls of the members, (2) the salvation of others, and (3) dedication to a devotion or a way of conducting the apostolate. Their charism did not lay only in the third element but in all three. Their purposes were decidedly religious and eschatological as well as incarnational. Today the eschatological has been replaced by an incarnational theology interpreted too secularistically and humanistically. Transcendent themes have been toned down in favor of a strong emphasis on egalitarian rights, on a type of justice interpreted not only as equity but as evenness, a kind of uniformity without differences. Everyone knows that only in unity is strength. But a doctrinaire egalitarianism sows an atomism and separatedness within a group, because it deems individual rights and desires more important than the group's religious cause and dream.

What we must recognize is that this excessive stress upon egalitarian and humanistic ideals is an ideology. It is one way — and only one way — of interpreting democracy and justice in society and in religious groups. To combat it is not to give up on democracy but to see it in another light and give it a different definition. How differently democracy can be interpreted was brought home to me a few years ago as I overheard a conversation between an American priest — a born-again egalitarian — and a young female member of the lay San Egidio community in Rome. She was describing how the community functioned and mentioned that in her particular community, because of its particular makeup and history, only particular men and no women were asked to speak at the prayer services. The American priest objected that this was a grave error, that it was supremely important, if not for her personally, as a symbol and sign to others, that women be allowed to preach in every community. She answered that the San Egidio community did not approach questions ideologically, but pragmatically. Some of the other communities did have women preachers, but because of its particular history and talents, her group preferred not to have them and she was happy with things as they were. She explained that for the San Egidio group three things were of paramount importance: (1) prayer together over the Word of God, (2) friendship or mutual support, and (3) work for and with the poor. All else must cede before the achievement of these goals. The American priest's voice rose in dictation announcing that she was wrong and that the American interpretation of women's rights was correct. But she stood her ground and deftly changed the subject.

We have come full circle in religious life. In the sixties, after many years of repression and an exaggerated supernaturalism we needed to put aside much useless regimentation of our own lives that had us walk in lockstep without touching our hearts or motivation. We had to recognize our duty before God to participate in building up a kingdom of justice and peace fighting for the civil rights of women and minorities. But this did not mean that such moral concerns should have become the cardinal and overriding program of religious congregations sweeping all else away in their wake. Now that both the lights and shadows of such emphases in religious life are coming into higher relief, we are at a better place to take stock and re-discover that our involvement with the world must begin beyond the world.

While the psychological agendas within religious life and the quasi-political agendas in our apostolates were very important, neither of them were the *unum necessarium.* If it is to be truly Christian, religious life must center upon that aspect of Christianity which relates our lives to the transcendent. It is on this side of the equation that religious life must seek its prophecy. It is in reminding people of the divine enchantment of the world that it will discover its essential mission. It is upon this that our reflection on reforming religious life must insist.

[4] *Religious Life Review*, vol. 30, Nov/Dec, 1991, pp. 284-291.

In her article "Religious Life and the Need for Salt,"[4] Joan Chittister asks the right questions regarding contemporary religious life. She begins with the wise affirmation that today, some 30 years since Vatican II, the project of providing self-expression to traditionally repressed religious and catering to their psychological needs has now been achieved. Those who clamor for freedom and dialogue are knocking on open doors. She says that we must now move to questions about the meaning of the group and how it can be prophetic in today's world in response to its founders' charism. She calls for passion. But her answers, giving her interpretation of prophecy, are still too tightly centered on concerns of ecology, social assistance and human rights. They remain within a "pragmatic" model of Christianity and seem but another reiteration of the program of liberal politics. As such they render true religious passion impossible. These liberal concerns are important and must be addressed by the Church — lay, clerical and religious. But addressing such issues, in my opinion, will not be the salvation of religious life, because its problems do not arise from a neglect of such matters. Its problem is not its lack of moral outreach in social, economic and ecological areas, but of religious centering, of realizing what the poor themselves realize and express in their popular religions, that my union with God through Jesus is central, that I must work at it and that it is primarily in this that I will be thoroughly counter-cultural. Which is more counter-cultural — to say, we must strive to save planet earth, or to say we truly believe that the dead are with God because Jesus resurrected from the dead, and that this makes all the difference?

These are hard sayings, and I would welcome a dialogue about them. I am sure I have not expressed them adequately but am convinced that they contain a large grain of truth. I am encouraged in uttering them by the swing in the interests of the young in both Europe and North America toward a mystical sense of religion. In the sixties the young were caught up in the humanistic values of psychology and sociology, but today's youth exhibit a great interest in mysticism, religious cults and movements, apparitions and healings, the afterlife, and even in reincarnation and the satanic. From such a turn, so deeply enmeshed in the esoteric and the irrational, we cannot automatically conclude that a new age of Christian faith is about to dawn. One thing, however, is certain, that many of our contemporaries are experiencing a deep void of meaning in an anorexic and bulimic world where money, notoriety, power, individualism and equality have become the primary values. Does not this turning signal that secular humanism, for all its ethical achievements, is lacking in profundity, does not pacify the restless heart, and has to a degree been an impoverishment? Does it not show that contemporary positivism is rooted in a failure of the religious imagination? Is it not a sign of the times when people living in sophisticated technological cultures begin to be attracted to religious beliefs interpreted in a most simplistic fashion?

I am aware of the ready responses to the distinction I draw within Christianity between morality and religion. Most will describe it as dualistic — for contemporary pundits the most damning of epithets. They will say that I am separating things that are essentially linked, that love of God and love of neighbor are inter-ingredient, two aspects of the same thing. If you do not care for the person you see, how can you say you love the God you do not see? Those who love God should find its primary expression in dedicating themselves entirely to caring for the neighbor, friend or enemy. Prayer is missionary and missionary activity is prayer — and on and on.

Others will say that I give a false description of the present situation of religious life, that it is not true that those who are engaged in social justice and ecology tend to pray less or are not interested in the transcendent or in sacraments or in the eschatological.

I know these rejoinders are partly true, but also that they are partly false. I know that the two aspects of Christianity, religion and morality, love of God and love of neighbor, are very closely intertwined and am aware of Karl Rahner's brilliant attempt to essentially conjoin them.[5] But I know too that they are conceptually distinct, because I have seen them separated in the history of the Church. At times, the Church has experienced the extreme of quietism, an over-emphasis on faith without good works, and other times, the heresy of action, a hectic involvement in important works of justice and charity, to the detriment of a life of faith, prayer and interiority, which is the very soul of the apostolate.

It is up to each of us to examine our life to determine where we are. But I am convinced that the problems of religious life stem only partly from a lack of adequate delivery systems or from an ignorance about psychology, social systemics, and anthropological models in an age of rapid change. I am convinced that their deeper source lies in the confusion between religion and morality and an insistence upon the latter because of a loss of faith and interest in the former.

If Catholicism is centered almost exclusively upon doing the moral good, upon promoting social justice and ecology or upon fighting pornography and abortion, then what is the meaning of its theological doctrines and dogmas? What is the meaning of the redemption through Christ for a religion reduced to morality? What is the meaning of the Eucharist? Are these dogmas and sacraments only stimuli for action, stories and symbols subtly swaying us to do what is truly important — fostering the construction of a socially just and ecologically sound world, creating the kingdom of morality? Are they but

[5] Cf. "Reflections on the Unity of the Love of Neighbour and the Love of God," *Theological Investigations*, Vol. II, Chap. 16. Baltimore, Helicon Press, 1969, pp. 231 ff.

13

religious accouterments? If so why not be honest and simply drop them? Is the Resurrection just a story whose real cash value is all those smaller resurrections which can occur in a society, in history, or in each human life?

How is a religious congregation which centers so strongly on morality to be differentiated from such groups as UNICEF or the FAO wherein men and women devote themselves to humanitarian causes at times for wages far less than they could obtain elsewhere?

Since Vatican II, theologians including Rahner and Schillebeeckx have highlighted the thesis that Christ is at work in the world wherever good is being done and humane causes fostered. Theologies have been advanced that interpret the work of building up the kingdom of God as primarily focused on our present life in the world, asserting that salvation is not only after death but begins here, that the glory of God is man (and woman) fully alive. I am in sympathy with such emphases and also with modern efforts to forge a new form of religious life dependent more on interpersonal dialogue than on impersonal regimentation, but must admit that neither effort by itself sets me on fire. And judging from vocation statistics of "progressive" congregations, upon which we will reflect in Chapter Three, I know that they have not stirred the young. The reason, I suspect, is because such emphases are profoundly incomplete and born in part from a loss of a lively faith in the transcendent. They are very well-intentioned and are aimed at responding to the criticisms of Christianity arising from the side of modern humanistic atheism. They are reflex reactions to the partial truths contained in the atheisms of Marx and Freud and Nietzsche, all of whom have accused Christianity of being the root cause of modern society's alienations. In the effort to meet these criticisms of these seminal thinkers various forms of incarnational theology have been developed which stress the co-partnership between God and humans in the world.

These theologies have not all been of equal value.

Some of them even diminish God's infinity in an effort to put humans on something of a par with the Godhead. Though I can sympathize with much of this, I believe that it has simply gone too far. We must certainly stress secondary causes and not run immediately to the primary Cause for answers to human problems. This is the doctrine of Thomas Aquinas himself. But Christianity demands a response to the world and to human existence different from that of contemporary humanism. While humanism focuses on human power and freedom, Christianity begins in a humble gratitude before a God from whom we receive even our power and freedom. One of its vital concerns is our inborn tendency to distort our freedom, arising from what Luther called the "incurvedness" of our will. We must never push to the background of our minds the fact that Christianity is about God and sin and the need for God's graceful hand to help us make proper use of our freedom.

Christian religion must be not only implicitly but explicitly about God and our relationship with God. It is from a union with God in prayer that will emanate the light on how we are to relate to God, the world, and each other. And if a life is to be devoted to religion in a special way, if it is to be a *consecrated religious* life, it must be lived primarily in view of this relationship to God, not only in ideal but also in structure. It must be constructed in such a way that the life of a group abets in its members this concern about the relationship to God and gives witness of it to others. Such a life steeped in personal prayer, dialogue about the faith, and community devotion as well as devotions, will produce something we may have lost, a solid number of holy men and women whose life has a deep center. If this is so, I am sure that young people will again be attracted to religious life, not so much because it is relevant or more interesting than the world, but for the simple reason that religious life so construed and so lived *is* what it purports to be — religious.

2. RELIGIOUS LIFE AND MODERNITY

In our attempt to take a second look at contemporary attempts at renewing religious life, it may be well to review more concretely the actual developments that have taken place since the last ecumenical council. My description is far from definitive and is presented with the greatest humility and in the hope of encouraging other descriptions and ongoing dialogue.

There are many ways of describing what has happened in the last 30 years since Vatican II. Historians say that there has been a shakeout after each ecumenical council and that approximately 25 or 30 years are required for the spirit of a Council to take root and bear its best fruit. Commentators on the development of religious life since Vatican II seem to concur on this. They now present this development in three stages: (1) the rigidity prior to Vatican II, (2) the immediate chaos after Vatican II, and (3) the current period of sober reassessment with its talk of refounding. Some students of contemporary religious life have named these stages Paradigm I, Paradigm II, and Paradigm III.

Vatican II was an effort in openness and *aggiornamento*. Its changes were radical. The Council recognized the ecclesial reality of other Christian religions, opened the way to dialogue with non-Christian religions, took a radically new position on religious freedom, realized the independent goodness of the secular world, and called for a renewal of the liturgy and of religious life, recognizing that through baptism the laity are called to the same degree of holiness as priests and religious.

All very heady at the time, exhilarating and in many
ways very positive and productive. Vatican II brought the
Church face-to-face with the world and urged it to view it
in its glory as well as its weakness. I do not think anyone
really wants to go back. But even Vatican II had its shadow
side. One of its results was that Catholicism in general and
religious life in particular seemed less important. When
personal conscience was exalted, when sin and hell were
de-emphasized in favor of love and heaven, when the great
enemies from Protestant theology were quoted side by side
with Rahner and Lonergan, when many distinctions were
blurred and the Catholic ghetto vanished — there was no
longer a dragon to kill. Now, while enemies, distinctions,
ghettos and dragons are not eminently desirable, they did
provide one thing: *identity*. Their removal was a major
reason why the principal question exercising religious
orders since Vatican II, has been *ad nauseam* the question
of identity. What does it mean to be a religious, a Jesuit, a
Dominican, a Franciscan, an Ursuline, a Daughter of St.
Paul?

But the identity-question had other non-ecclesiastical
sources. The post-Vatican II world found itself engulfed in a
cultural upheaval that the Council had not caused.
Religious congregations were not simply surrounded by a
materialistic and skeptical culture, they were immersed in
it. It had infiltrated the convent walls. J.M.R. Tillard, O.P.
says that the failure of religious life is a failure in
enthusiasm, passion, and wholeheartedness and is rooted
in a shift in belief, a hesitancy of faith. Theologian Walter
Kasper has remarked that what we encounter today is not
only an external atheism, but an atheism within our own
hearts.

Cultural modernity has been analyzed and
reanalyzed as the onslaught of secularization.[1] It was as if
in the second half of our century the Enlightenment had
reached the masses. What up to the present were ideas of
intellectuals, philosophers and cranky atheists, now, due to
better communication and general education, became the

[1] In support of a minority dissenting position, see Andrew Greenback and Michael Hout, "The Secularization Myth," *The Tablet*, June 10, 1989, pp. 665-667.

fabric of culture at large. The well-documented cultural
revolution which has been playing itself out since the
1960's seemed to be a quantitative expansion of ideas
which had been around since the 18th century.

But Paul Ricoeur underlines that the Enlightenment
has gone through two distinct stages. For our purposes, we
will speak of a first and second Enlightenment, that of the
17th and 18th centuries and the different one which began
in the 19th and flowered in the 20th century.

Both began with doubt, methodic doubt, but the first
went back to consciousness and found certitude, while the
second in returning to consciousness found only suspicion.
Descartes began by doubting everything methodically, but
banished doubt because he believed we could find a place
of certitude in consciousness. Even doubting was a form of
thinking, and the one thing I could not doubt was that "I
think." *Cogito, ergo sum.* At the center of consciousness
there was clarity and distinctness (*les idées claires et
distinctes*), a way of banishing skepticism about the
existence of the world or the truth of morality. Thus the first
Enlightenment was characterized by an overconfidence in
a certain type of reason and an exaltation of human
consciousness. Its champion was Kant for whom the
subject became a partial creator of the object known.

But the second Enlightenment grounded in Marx,
Freud and Nietzsche, was quite different. Commencing
similarly from scientific methodical doubt, these thinkers
returned to the conscious and thinking subject but found
there not a place of certitude but another ground for
suspicion. For them human consciousness turned out to be
a creator of illusions, the fabricator of masks, the great
pretender. Consciousness itself was in need of unmasking.
This is the case especially when it concocts religion.
Religion was the deception par excellence. It was an
opium creating lassitude among oppressed peoples (Marx),
it was a collective obsessive neurosis (Freud), a cover for
the will to power of the weak and the envious (Nietzsche).
Leaving aside the fine nuances present in their systems, we

can say that for these thinkers consciousness spins illusory language about God to hide what men and women really desire: sexual gratification, wealth and power.

This modern atheism, the atheism of consciousness as pretender, has with legitimacy been called a "beautiful" atheism. It has an ethical side and bears a moral attraction. It is born of the desire to avoid masks and pretensions. The modern atheist is an atheist because he does not want to remain within a false consciousness. He wants to be honest; he does not want to tell a lie. The great modern drive, the drive of the second Enlightenment, is to be authentic, not to worship an idol. For this reason, too, its geniuses, Freud, Marx and Nietzsche can present themselves as moralists. This is why Sartre, following Nietzsche, can present belief in God as bad faith. As described in the second Enlightenment, consciousness is the escape artist, the artful dodger. A consciousness so construed attains salvation when it strives to catch itself at its own artifices.

In light of this we can explain two moral phenomena which have occurred in our lifetime. First, the fact that, for many people of the 20th century, hypocrisy became the great sin and sincerity the great virtue. It was hypocrisy not to admit who and what you were. If you were gay, you must say it. If you were committing adultery, you must admit it. Being moral meant coming out of various closets. But unfortunately many people failed to ask the question whether acting out according to the instincts of these closets was good or bad. Some decided that anything was allowed as long as you owned up to it. Still others, plagued by secret guilt, tried to get everyone else to approve what they were doing privately; they wanted their private morality publicly sanctioned.

The other phenomenon characteristic of the second Enlightenment was that contemporary thinkers were more interested in meaning than in truth. This explains the death of apologetics in the last 30 years. Hugo Meynell bemoans the fact that the last real apologist was C.S. Lewis. Today, he complains, theologians are more concerned to show that Christianity is relevant. What floods the market is writing on the social and political implications of Christianity, or on its power to lead us to a fuller and more authentic personal life. Admitting the importance of such writing, he believes, nevertheless that a serious apologetic that looks beyond meaning to truth is absolutely indispensable for the Church and that many of its present ills are due to a neglect of it. Without an apologetic, says Meynell, "the unbeliever is apt to infer that educated Christians have really grasped the fact that social reform, political action, and psychic hygiene are that to which religious aspiration ought to be directed."[2]

Related to this move from truth to meaning is the fact that for the last 20 years seminarians, both religious and diocesan, have uncharacteristically manifested a distaste for intellectual argument. Even some of the most intelligent tended to shun involvement in debates about the truth and falsity of moral positions or thorny dogmatic issues like the interpretation of the Resurrection, and were satisfied if they were convinced that a particular Church doctrine held some meaning for people. More and more religious showed up on the Myers-Briggs test as feelers and not thinkers. Brought up in an Enlightenment of suspicion, they suspected intestinally that the search for truth is impossible and that the different philosophies are simply a parade of ideologies with no criterion for deciding which is right and which is wrong. This is probably the deep side of the vocation crisis among the youth of the second Enlightenment. If consciousness suspects its very self, how can it commit itself to anything for a long-term future?

Ricoeur believes that we must face head-on what he calls the "hermeneutics of suspicion." We must take seriously its originators and thinkers. We cannot return to a primitive naiveté. But he also insists that we cannot remain in a state of denial, in a vacuum of truth, in mere negation; we must move to a new place of affirmation. To do this we must not only respect the creators of suspicion but also

[2] "Faith and Reason," *The Tablet*, March 11, 1989, p. 276.

question them. We must suspect the suspicioners and put them to the test. We must transcend the Enlightenment in both its phases.

We will not achieve this by attempting to return to consciousness conceived of as pure thought, to a thinking self which is sufficient unto itself apart from the world. For contemporary philosophers such a move is impossible. Consciousness can only be encountered as already *in* and *of* the world. The only way to discover what the human mind or human consciousness is like is through an examination of the works it has strewn in the world down the centuries, that is, through an examination of the institutions and documents of culture. Ricoeur bets that after such a reflection the scandal of the cross will remain as much a scandal for modern consciousness as it was for an earlier consciousness. He bets that the scandal of the cross is transcultural, a scandal not merely for humans in one stage of history but for the human condition as such.

For the modern age, theology's method has itself changed. We do not go immediately to the transcendent, to God, to the sacred and then try to relate God to the world. We find God through the world; we discover the transcendent as the depth of the world. We seek an incarnational approach to eschatology and transcendence. We try to find God within the world as the Creative Moment therein, as the source without which justice and equality, as absolute moral imperatives, lack motivation and a rational ground.

The Enlightenment and the Re-definition of Religious Life

Whether we consider it in its first or second phase, the Enlightenment is marked by the same ideals, the dethroning of authority and tradition in favor of reason, free thought, and humanistic brotherhood. The ideals of both Enlightenments can be summarized most easily in the slogan of the French Revolution whose 200th anniversary we celebrated in 1989: liberty, fraternity, and equality.

It was onto these very three ideals that religious life fastened almost in sequence during our lifetime in an effort to redefine itself, to forge a new identity. It had to deal with them as reinforced by the genius of Nietzsche, Freud and Marx. Note that these ideals are mirror-imaged in the three vows, and are in a sense the concern of the vows: (liberty) obedience, (fraternity) chastity, and (equality) poverty.

The first of the Enlightenment ideals to make dramatic entrance into our culture and religious life was the ideal of personal or individual freedom (its hero, Nietzsche). Never in a general culture had the notion "I want x" enjoyed such power as a reason for morally justifying an action. In an earlier climate of opinion, the fact that someone strongly desired something rendered suspect his or her opinion about it. In this earlier climate it was because an issue like abortion was so important that it could not be decided by the person who was subjectively involved. She could hardly have an objective viewpoint. But now it was precisely *because* an issue was so important that it must be left up to individual choice. Major books have been written documenting and decrying this shift to individualistic freedom: Alasdair McIntyre's *After Virtue*, Allan Bloom's *The Closing of the American Mind*, and Robert Bellah's *Habits of the Heart*. Some of its critics distinguish between a liberal spirit which is admirable in its pursuit of discussion and exchange of ideas, and a liberal dogma which in its exaggerations is pernicious because it has not allowed us to build a community upon agreed societal values.

Contemporary American democracy has many facets of greatness. Unlike the French and Russian Revolutions, which ended in reigns of terror or totalitarianism, the American Revolution alone succeeded in producing a truly representative democracy of the people. In the 20th century, the United States has been the locus of many positive social revolutions in the areas of racism and sexism. In this way, it has been a pathfinder to the world, making trial runs that other Western nations are just now beginning to imitate. Its greatness lies, however, not in the arbitrary or whimsical freedom that has recently developed within its borders, but in its assumption of many responsibilities, in its willingness to sacrifice the fulfillment of personal desires for the sake of the benefit of others. It asks its people to suppress any impulse to reject or subjugate those whose color or sex or religion is different from theirs. It demands that they follow the rule of law and due process granting even the most hardened criminal the presumption of innocence and a fair trial. Whatever America possesses of greatness and dignity is not born of a binge of freedom. It rises primarily out of sacrifice undergone for the purpose of preserving profound human values. Her greatness lies in respecting sinners even while denouncing their sins.

An arbitrary type of freedom, an exaggeration of the freedoms born of the Enlightenment, invaded American society and religious life in the 1960's and early 1970's. The major concern of religious and seminarians of that era was self-fulfillment and the idea that they could not be fulfilled unless they made their own choices about lifestyle and ministry. This was also the age when seminarians, the world over, simply cast off rules that had been sacrosanct for years, refused to kneel down in chapel and to acknowledge any difference of status between themselves and their professors. Their slogan was that of the youth culture of the 1960's: "Don't trust anyone over thirty!" Articles on religious obedience appearing in the *Review for Religious* at the time, had less to do with recognizing the superior's authority as God's representative or as the leader of a group engaged in a religious cause, than with how he or she should be a caring person attentive to the needs of community members. The commands of obedience were replaced by talk of accompaniment. Superiors gave way to coordinators who ruled by consensus and were skilled in the principles of subsidiarity and collegiality.

The second ideal of the Enlightenment used in the attempted re-definition of religious life was that of fraternity, now interpreted as intimacy (its hero: Freud; its favorite book, Fromm's *Art of Loving*). In the late 1960's and early 1970's fraternity came to the fore in the form of the felt-need for intimacy and community. Some felt that religion itself was a projection of affective needs. Everyone seemed sure that, without at least psychological sexual relations, you could not really develop as a person. A good number of priests and religious abandoned their vowed commitment while they were still nubile in the conviction that the Church would soon wake up and change the rules. Others adopted what for a brief time was called the "third way," that is, remaining somewhat chaste and celibate while dating. All of this was later exacerbated by the gay movement and the inability of some to realize that, whatever one might think of homoerotic relations in general, all religious, whether homosexually or heterosexually oriented, had taken the same vow.

Those who chose to remain and to keep the vows fought for a more fraternal and intimate form of community life and began using the word "sharing" as an intransitive verb. "Sharing" went on till the wee hours of the morning. "Thanks for sharing" and a big hug seemed to end every conversation, even a conversation in which a provincial in no uncertain terms had said, "No!"

For all its positive aspects, this age of individualistic freedom and of fraternity/intimacy/community, was an "era of the divided heart." It was a time, not entirely past, in which many of us, all of us to some degree, were *sidetracked*, distracted, not completely present to the task, unhappy. For a good number the religious life became an avocation rather than a vocation. They did good work and were not uninterested in the religious community, but their treasure, their compelling interest seemed to be elsewhere. They did not realize it at the time and cannot be blamed, but absorbed in themselves and their personal projects or affective needs, jettisoning traditional practices without replacing them with new communal structures, they were sapping the energy of the group.

It was in subconscious reaction to this drift that there appeared in religious-life circles the talk about the need for a shared vision or a common sense of mission. Much effort went into writing mission statements which everyone signed and accepted mutteringly in paraliturgical ceremonies. But there was an unexamined assumption in writing such mission declarations, the assumption that everyone desired a common vision. Though there has always been a degree of pluralism and confusion in the Church, what seemed different now was that some religious seemed almost to welcome the confusion. They gave up on the search for a shared vision not simply because it was hard to attain, but because in a deep sense they did not want one. It may be a hard saying, but I believe it is true that many of us, all of us to some degree, did not desire a true unity of mind and vision, at least not one which was set down in great detail, one which invaded and interfered with our life.

The third ideal of the French Revolution and Enlightenment to enter religious life in the time of attempted re-definition was that of equality (its hero, Marx). It was the same ideal which gave rise to liberation theology and to the preferential option for the poor. It came strongly to the fore in the 1980's. Beginning with the 32nd General Congregation of Jesuits it thundered into religious life under the title of faith and justice. Social analysis and peace-and-justice committees soon became the vogue. Religious, male and female, left long-standing apostolates in education and hospitals and went to work among the poor and oppressed of both the third and first worlds. Soon the movement became involved with justice questions within the Church as well as the world, in the first as well as the third world. Now suddenly every question was interpreted in terms of the power-equality schema. Everywhere there was talk of the need for assertiveness, the tactics of confrontation, the evil of patriarchy, the *lucha de clases*. Not just politics but a liberal politics was brought to the center of religion and religious life. At Boston College in

1984 the Jesuit historian John Padberg said, "It must be admitted that from a historical point of view many of the changes which have taken place in feminine religious communities do not derive from Vatican II, but from the secular feminist movement."

I believe that all of these attempted re-definitions of religious life have failed because religious have remained at a superficial level in thinking of freedom, fraternity and equality. In their general thrust these new values are wonderful and exhilarating and are here to stay. But they must be retrieved in their Christian depth and meaning.

Secularization and the Return of Religion

We are in a polarization situation in the Church today, liberals against conservatives. This can be documented by reading any theological review or religious newspaper. Avery Dulles, in fact, discerns four quasi-ideologies in the Church: liberal, traditionalist, neo-conservative, and radical.[3] Signs of the resistance to liberal secularism appear not only in a growing fundamentalism in Church practice, but in the "postliberal" or "postmodern" stances in academic theology championed by authors like George Lindbeck, Huston Smith, and Stanley Hauerwas. The resistance is also apparent in the area of religious and priestly vocations. In the entire industrialized world it is the progressive congregations which continue to experience a decline, while conservative congregations enjoy substantial increases.

[3] See "Catholicism and American Culture," *America*, January 27, 1990, pp. 54-59.

But what is not understood is that the very fact of polarization has a religious meaning. It means that modernity cannot be understood as a single phenomenon of ongoing secularization. Something else is also occurring. The evident resistance to liberal secularism hints at the possibility of a great reversal, a move to a higher synthesis.

Many are willing to see a religious significance in secularization. They interpret it as the desire to be authentic, to be rid of idols, to avoid at all costs the telling of a lie. But is there not also a deep meaning to the liberal/ conservative split and the rise of fundamentalism and neo-conservatism? Is this not also a sign of the times? It seems simplistic to view the resistance to tendencies which have been the vogue since Vatican II as a mere knee-jerk reaction, a neurotic flight to security in the face of a secularized world. The fact of these counter-movements has a religious sense. It reveals, among other things, that modern men and women still recognize the presence of mystery and transcendence and feel that without it liberty, fraternity, and equality remain superficial and, in the end, stifling.

In an article entitled "Can the West be Converted?", Leslie Newbigin, the famous Anglican missionary to India, asks: Can there be an effective missionary encounter with *this* culture — this so powerful, persuasive, and confident culture which (at least until very recently) simply regarded itself as "the coming world civilization"?

He bemoans as excessive the criticism of the 19th-century missionary movement on the part of socially-minded Christians, and disagrees with dropping the term "foreign missions" in favor of "overseas ministries" or "cross-cultural ministry." Says Newbigin: "The contemporary embarrassment about the missionary movement of the previous century is not as we like to think, evidence that we have become more humble. It is, I fear, much more clearly evidence of a shift in belief. It is evidence that we are less ready to affirm the uniqueness, the centrality, the decisiveness of Jesus Christ as universal Lord and Savior, the Way by following whom the world is to be tested, the Life in whom alone life in its fullness is to be found."[4]

Instead of weighing the Christian religious experience in the scale of reason as our culture understands reason, let us suppose, says Newbigin, that the Gospel is true; that, in the story of the Bible and in the life and death and resurrection of Jesus, the Creator and Lord of the universe has actually manifested himself to declare and effect his

[4] *International Bulletin of Missionary Research,* April 1988, p. 51.

purpose; and that, therefore, everything else, including all the actions and assumptions of our culture, has to be assessed and can only be validly assessed in the scales which this revelation provides. What would it mean if, instead of trying to understand the Gospel from the point of view of our culture, we tried to understand our culture from the point of view of the Gospel?

Rabbi Abraham Heschel said something similar when addressing a group of theologians at a conference on the future of theology: "It has always seemed puzzling to me how greatly attached to the Bible you seem to be and yet how much like pagans you handle it. The great challenge to those of us who wish to take the Bible seriously is to let it teach us its own essential categories; and then for us to think *with* them, instead of just *about* them."[5]

Something new is stirring, something new striving to be born. A significant group of theologians is reaching for a post-liberal stance which might nourish the hunger for truth and deeper meaning which exists in America. Professor Huston Smith puts it as follows: "While the West's 'brain,' which for present purposes we can equate with the modern university, rolls ever further down the reductionistic path, other centers of society — our emotions, for example, as they find expression through our artists and our wills — protest. These other centers of our selves feel they are being dragged, kicking and screaming, down an ever-darkening tunnel."[6]

The first world turns to suicide, drugs and hooliganism and graffiti because of a lack of meaning in the lives of its members. Culture is the meaning system of society. According to some sociologists, religion is the deepest aspect of that meaning system. But the religion which remains in Western society is impoverished. The religion of our secularized cultures is highly intellectualized, pared down, devoid of mystery and passion. Mysteries are embarrassments and are explained away reductively. Modern churches look like banks. Statues are either banished or shrunken to stand sheepishly

[5] Quoted by Prof. Albert Outler, "Toward a Post-liberal Hermeneutics," *Theology Today*, October 1985, p. 290.

[6] *Toward the Post-Modern Mind*, Crossroad, 1982, p. 25.

in shadowy corners. The ardent devotion so apparent in the popular religion of an earlier immigrant Church has given way to a purist starkness as well as a wordiness in liturgy. Little remains of the sense of mystery and mysticism, of an invisible reality beyond the material one, of Blake's "infinity in a grain of sand" and "eternity in an hour."

And what has sprung up in the desert of modernity? The so-called "pipeline religion" of charismatics and Pentecostals, a revival of a more emotional form of prayer with a need for a personal attachment to Jesus, expressed emotionally and publicly, the ministry of healing — in sum the desire for a backdrop to life, a deeper dimension, an invisible world; the need once again to feel for a God who is transcendent as well as immanent. The pendulum swings of the Christological debates of the early Church are again in evidence. We desire the divine face of Jesus as well as the human face of God.

The third re-definition of religious life in terms of equality and justice is an improvement over the first two re-definitions in terms of liberty and fraternity, especially if they are interpreted as individualistic freedom and a sentimentalized intimacy/community. Individualism cannot form community. Nor can we religious be merely *intimiste* in our spirituality. We cannot be satisfied with simply voicing our affections of love toward others or even toward the Lord. We must step out and do something. Love must also be active, social, and even political. Christians cannot concentrate solely on their own salvation whether earthly or celestial. "What would the Lord say," asked Charles Peguy, "if we go to him without all the others?"

On the other hand, this third effort to redefine ourselves and discover a lost identity was (is) in some ways more seductive, more liable to become an idol, for in itself it is strongly rooted in the Gospel and demands great sacrifice. The quest for social justice is "a constitutive part" of the Gospel, said an oft-quoted text of the 1971 Synod of Bishops. But it, too, has its shadow-side. It was an improvement because it took the focus off of the individual-subject, the I, but it was not sufficient because it replaced the individual subject with another earthly subject, the species-subject, Marx's *Gattungswesen*, or with a part of society, the poor, the oppressed of the human species. To define religious life *principally* in terms of social justice is to make the Marxian move of replacing religion with the need to foster a truly socialized man and woman. We will develop this idea further in Chapter Four.

While fear of idolatry caused men of earlier ages to set God above the world and beyond all images, the danger of idolatry returns a hundredfold when we look for God within the bowels of the world.

Some will call this double-talk and say they will have nothing to do with a religion which does not work ardently for liberation, equality, compassion, and the betterment of people. But such a conclusion does not follow from what I am saying. Just the opposite is true. Unless we live in light of the truth that the world belongs to God and that its primary duty is to praise him in gratitude for what has been given, we cannot even begin to construct a world of justice. Unless we see that God is first and creator and that the human is second and created, we cannot find a solid basis for human equality or for treating everyone with justice and care.

Evolutionists turned philosophers say that humans are equal only by the accident that a group of beings with about the same size brain flowered at a certain period of time. As a result these thinkers can find no ground for the moral imperative of justice. Such an imperative appears only when and if we view humans as having a relationship to an Absolute whose essence is Love. Humans have a dignity not because they happen to have a complex brain which gives them a kind of free will, but because they are loved and because the very meaning of their being is to love as the Father loves. As Martin Buber has said, whoever makes freedom the primary characteristic of humans is blind to the real nature of human existence which is "being sent and a being commissioned."[7]

[7] Martin Buber, *The Eclipse of God,* Harper and Row, 1962, p. 69.

31

It is because God's love for us does not rise out of a personal need but is gratuitous, that the universe has meaning and that social justice is an imperative. In this discovery we will find true freedom. For the God of the absolute future is a God of plenitude who does not enslave nor brook enslavement.

Contemporary thinkers are obsessed by the thought that dualisms must be overcome at all cost, that all distinctions must be leveled, the natural and the supernatural, laity and clergy, Church and world. In this same vein, because of the doctrine that all are called to the same degree of holiness in baptism, they tend to believe that the distinction between laity and religious cannot ultimately be maintained. But in counteracting dualisms we must be careful not to submerge certain important distinctions. There may be other distinctions between religious life and lay life which are not connected with the call to holiness shared in baptism.

Religious, I believe, are called to a different kind of separation from the world. Religious must not be above or beyond the world, nor seek to escape its toils. But *yes*, their life must be distinct and separate by taking up the very different lifestyle of a pilgrim as did the apostles, not remaining at home but accompanying Jesus on the way. Both J.M.R. Tillard and Marcello Azevedo define religious life as a particular way of following Jesus, one that involves the choice of a particular existential form of life. This form of life is inspired by that group of disciples of the Gospel, like Peter and Andrew, who desired to follow Jesus in his actual journeys in Galilee and Judea.

They were different from those who stayed home, like Joseph of Arimathea and Nicodemus. It is not clear that Peter and Andrew were holier than Joseph and Nicodemus, says Tillard. In fact there is some evidence they were less so, for at least they did not deny Jesus as Peter did. Yet they did adhere to Jesus in a different way. The discipleship of Peter and Andrew was more explicit and direct and public. They made Christ and his goals their profession and their career. His actions and ways altered more dramatically the concrete shape of their lives.

Again, if a religious is supposed to be a prophet in today's world, as many commentators urge, then he or she must be different from others in the way that a prophet is different from those to whom he or she prophesies. The prophet is one who shows the way. Religious must teach by their life that all Christians must be *in* the world but not *of* the world, that their greatness will not spring from surrender to the values of the world. Without a distinction between religious and laity the significance and identity of a truly Christian laity may also be in danger of being lost.

"The religious," says Tillard, "challenges the idolatry of progress by his own existence, which as a rule is dedicated to a work of humanization . . . he proclaims that humanization of the world fits into a plan that extends far beyond it. And he declares that the human heart can fulfill its hope only by welcoming the One who is the bearer of that plan."[8]

[8] *A Gospel Path: The Religious Life*, Brussels, Lumen Vitae, 1978, p. 39.

Something new is being born: a higher synthesis. It will consist essentially in a re-winning for human consciousness of the sense of the transcendent and a new understanding of what is meant by a separation from the world. The problem of the third world is poverty; the problem of the first world is paganism. The third world retains the sense of the transcendent, though the embrace may at times be cluttered with emotion and superstitions and not translate into social action. The first world has in many cases simply given up the embrace. And in doing so it finds no adequate ground for love of neighbor, enemy, or stranger.

Earlier spirituality taught that only in recognizing God's sovereignty can we avoid pride. It is through the same recognition that we will become compassionate and work for justice. True *kenosis* lies in the realization that all humans — poor or rich, woman or man, ourselves or others — are of secondary importance. What is of prime importance is beyond. But the God beyond sends us back to the world whose inhabitants he loves unconditionally as individual persons and as societies and places upon us the moral imperative of justice and the command of love. Through a relationship with the Lord established in prayer, the extent of our task as Christians will be revealed. In transcendence we will rediscover immanence. Modernity and its religious need again to ponder the words of the psalmist: "In *your* light we shall see light."

3. VOCATIONS AND THE LAICIZATION OF RELIGIOUS LIFE

One of the most discussed aspects of contemporary religious life is its evident inability to attract new adherents who will carry the congregation into the 21st century. When people ask, "How is your congregation doing?" they almost always refer to success or failure in the area of vocations. We will deal with the vocation question twice in this book, here and in the final chapter, from two different but related points of view. Here we will look into the recent past and search out causes, there we will look to possibilities for the future.

The contemporary problem of religious vocations is very difficult to discuss because it requires drawing attention to painful statistics. One must allude to the median age of a congregation and face the fact that, if nothing changes, some congregations may die. Raymond Hostie, S.J., tells us in *La vie et la mort des ordres religieux* that three fourths of all Catholic religious congregations have faded into obscurity and that of some 105 foundations dating from before 1600, only 25 still exist. The examples of longevity are the exception. The vocation question is difficult, too, because there is so much pent-up resentment in religious congregations. Many religious are so resentful of the infantilism of the past, due to an arbitrary limitation on freedom and responsibility, that any hint that recent attempts at modernization may have been ill-conceived is met with impatience, passion and anger.

And really what can one say about vocations? That

one should try harder to attract them? But the very effort is enigmatic. The matter of vocations as it presents itself today seems to be out of our hands; it is an affair of the culture. As we have now heard *ad nauseam* a qualitative change occurred in the 1960's and 1970's. Negatively put, the world became overly secularized, and the supernatural was cast aside in favor of a materialism and a notion of freedom interpreted superficially as self-determination and individualism. There is, of course, a more positive and deeper interpretation of secularization as a hunger for authenticity and a repudiation of masks. But whatever the interpretation, one fact remains: Suddenly, within the first world religious vocations dried up — without warning. Who in the 1950's expected the 1960's? And because this decline in vocations appeared practically everywhere and in every congregation, it is difficult to present simple remedies, to blame ourselves for not having prayed or worked hard enough, or for not having been a little more obedient or somewhat poorer in our lifestyles. The vocation issue is part of a larger fabric. It is a cultural question and its definitive solution may demand another dramatic cultural shift. But changes of culture are out of our hands; they are in the hands of history, and history is in the hands of God.

It is my conviction, on the other hand, that though there is little evidence of another major cultural shift, there is something new at play in the area of vocations that may help us to decipher the cause of the decline and to work out a long-term approach to a solution.

Let us begin with certain new and indisputable facts. It is a fact that, for several years now, certain congregations have begun to enjoy vocations in large numbers, while others still attract only a paltry few. Another fact: It is the congregations which have changed in a dramatically "progressive" direction that still remain in a state of shock. These congregations do attract some vocations in the third world, but I am not aware of even one "progressive" congregation which is presently experiencing a general success in vocational recruitment in the first world. On the other hand there are certain more conservative congregations who are attracting significant numbers of vocations in the first world.

I hesitate to mention these facts because I know that rigid conservatives will pounce upon them immediately and say that the solution is evident: renounce all the tinkerings of modernism and return to a more literal reading and living of the disciplines and the traditions. I believe that such a response is not only naive but also a repudiation of the authority and inspiration of the Second Vatican Council. The call to *aggiornamento* is from the Holy Spirit, and it must continue.

But is there something to be learned from this difference between two types of congregations in the ability to attract vocations in the modern world? Progressive sisters with whom I have discussed these differences attribute the success of the conservative congregations to two things: (1) they recruit vocations at an early and impressionable age, and (2) certain dependent types need to join a group which offers them certitude and stability in the rigid adherence to traditional doctrines and rules. On the contrary, they add, the vocations attracted by the more progressive congregations, though few, tend to be older, more independent and mature, and will provide better leadership for the Church of the future.

But I wonder whether these explanations based on considerations of certitude, feelings of insecurity and dependence really go to the heart of the matter. It is true that in such a rapidly changing world there will be the temptation to escape into a milieu of certitude and absolutes, to look for a solid place to stand. Shifting sand is the soil of fundamentalism. It may also be true that the few vocations attracted to the more progressive groups are truly more mature and responsible, and that they ultimately may do more for the Kingdom. It is furthermore possible that the decline in vocations in these congregations is only a transitory phenomenon that will disappear as young people become accustomed to different forms of religious living and these groups themselves settle into a relative stability. The appeal of the newer, more conservative congregations may begin to diminish once the founders pass on and the enthusiasm begins to flag. Only time will tell.

But I also wonder whether the loss of vocations in general does not stem from deeper reasons, from what I will call a "laicization of religious life" resulting from a failure to seize the real nature of the renewal which was needed. I wonder, too, whether those congregations which have turned the corner have done so because, despite defects arising out of a too rigid conservatism, they have willy-nilly stemmed the process of laicization. Could it not be that in the admirable desire to affirm the intrinsic value of the secular world, to maximize individual freedom, and most of all to foster an egalitarianism in the Church, we have been led in practice to affirm the proposition that there is little or no difference between lay and religious life? No difference, that is, between a Christian life in the world and "the religious life" which demands, in all its forms a degree of "separation" from the world? It is evident that I am using the word "lay" as roughly synonymous with "secular" and not in its opposition to "clerical," which defines those in holy orders. There are, of course, many religious communities without priests.

I am convinced that the key to the vocation riddle lies here. The following is a tentative attempt to spur a dialogue through which our understanding of religious life may be enriched.

Religious life has traditionally been presented as "a state of perfection," as a higher way, as the way of perfect charity. Indeed, even Vatican II uses the phrase *Perfectae Caritatis* ("Of Perfect Charity") as the title of its treatise on the renewal of religious life. But many authors now insist that we must not draw any hierarchical distinction between religious and lay life. There is no order of priority. The call to holiness is universal since it is written into our baptism, since sanctity is possible in both ways of life, and since lay persons can often exhibit greater holiness and charity, not to speak of psychological wholeness, than do religious.

All of which is true, but is it totally relevant?

Certainly from most points of view the blurring of the distinction was a welcome relief. It was another aspect of the general rejection of the triumphalism that had infected the institutional Church, the repudiation of artificiality, of titles, of the sense of self-inflation. It was part of the call to religious to return to an evangelical humility, to the simple straw of the Gospel.

But the flattening of differences has also had other repercussions. Many traditions which flowed from the distinction and which acted as symbols to keep it alive were cast aside. Religious habits were often set aside as pretentious; many community prayer practices, as repetitive and boring; set schedules, as preventing members from the far more important work in the world. Distinctions between the "sacred" space of the cloister and the "profane" space of the world were banished as quaint and eccentric. Gone was the priority of the liturgical calendar over the world calendar. Gone was much of the sense of sacred time and sacred space and sacred persons consecrated in a special way to something which transcended the world.

My point is not that we must return to all of the practices and structures that have been dropped. Far from it. It is, rather, that these practices were vehicles carrying the sacred of the congregation and its myth, symbols which gave flesh to its intentionality and its charism. They incarnated and lent support to the spirituality of the congregation. They cannot be simply dropped without being in some way replaced. A religious congregation cannot just intellectually propound a vision or charism and leave it to each individual to discover a personal way of living it out. "Religious community is not simply a collection of Christians in search of personal perfection" says a document on community recently issued by the Congregation of Religious in preparation for the Synod on

Religious Life in autumn of 1994. It goes on to explain that "Religious community, in its structure, motivations, and distinguishing values, makes publicly visible and continually perceptible the gift of fraternity given by Christ to the whole Church. For this very reason, it has as its commitment and mission, which cannot be renounced, both to be and to be seen as a living organism of intense fraternal communion, a sign and a stimulus for all the baptized."[1] It is not a merely charismatic or prophetic entity, but also a political and social one. It must witness not only through the life of each individual, but as a social body, as an institution, as a structure in the life of the Church. And in order to achieve this it must have a social life of prayer as well as a personal one. It is only when a congregation offers this common life as a political and social countersign to the world that it will again attract vocations.

Aggiornamento does not mean, then, simply shedding; it must also involve the creating of new practices, new structures, new symbols which re-express a congregation in a way which is faithful to the past and yet in harmony with the valid insights of the modern world. Renewal should not discard, but through a rethinking preserve and give new expression to the distinction between "the religious life" and a life lived religiously in the world.

We are at the heart of the matter. What is the difference between "the religious life" and "a life that is religious"? Certainly everyone is called to live his or life religiously. The religious dimension, the dimension of the holy, must be the ultimate context of everyone's life. "Ultimate" because religious considerations must in the last analysis override all other considerations of art, pleasure, patriotism, and other human values. One who enters the religious life, however, makes religion not only the context of his life, but also its career. For it is one thing to observe the evangelical counsels as counsels, as all Christians should, and quite another thing to oblige oneself formally

[1] *Fraternal Life in Community,* Rome, St. Paul Books and Media, 1994, pp. 12, 13.

and publicly to observe them by *vows*. In making religion their career, their profession, religious adopt a religious form of life. Their religious vows, as well as the structures and practices of their life are all explicitly aimed at giving witness to what transcends the world. In the case of the lay person, it is the context of a career that is religious, but not the career itself. The life of the religious is different in that the career as well as the context is religious. Through the form of life which they espouse, they witness to the ultimate unimportance of things that are very important: human affection, freedom, and material comfort.

"If I were asked to designate the foundation of the religious life," says J.M.R. Tillard, "I would simply say that it is the whole of the Gospel — the charter of Christian existence as such — but seen from the angle of its radicalness."[2] The religious life is not distinguished from other Christian lives by a striving for perfection, nor even by adherence to the evangelical counsels, for all Christians are in some degree called to both of these. The radicalness which characterizes the religious life is found in a special existential style, a commitment to a way of life which in its content signifies clearly and publicly that for this group Jesus is "the one thing necessary."

In the words of *Lumen Gentium*, "The religious state constitutes a closer imitation and abiding re-enactment in the Church of the form of life which the Son of God made his own when he came into the world to do the will of the Father and which he propounded to the disciples who followed him" (No. 44). If the life of a vowed religious man is not a closer and more concrete re-enactment of the life of Christ, and as such a clear sign of contradiction to even the good things in the world, then he has in a sense stepped out of his vocation into lay life. He has lost his vocation. My question is whether whole congregations cannot in a sense lose their vocation, return to lay life and as a result lose their true identity. As such they appear to drift aimlessly and hold little power to attract, for they fail to present an important alternative to Christian life in the world.

[2] *A Gospel Path: The Religious Life*, Brussels, Lumen Vitae, 1978, p. 24.

It is interesting that *Lumen Gentium*, the Second Vatican Council's Constitution on the Church, makes its first mention of the religious life immediately after the paragraph on martyrdom and as a quasi-extension of it. This life may have attracted many dependent types, but it also attracted many persons so filled with love and idealism that they dared to be different, to resist the peer pressure of being thought odd, and to follow Jesus in a more literal way by leaving family, home and, at times, even country.

Possibly religious life as lived in certain congregations has ceased to attract the idealistic because the members of these congregations give little evidence of the radicality of the Gospel and of a deep interior life. Karl Rahner accepted the demise of the religious life as we knew it, but only in the hope of a new spirituality: "That rather bourgeois-chequered spirituality which was found — to outward appearances at least — in the orders before the first world war and which influenced religious life too much, may belong to the past and the young may say that it is useless from the start. But a new spirituality in religious life and in the Church will be assured of a real future."[3] But has the new spirituality in the form of a rich interior life embodied in a new form of observance actually unfolded?

Most congregations which have followed a progressive path are filled with two types of members. There are the more conservative ones who still adhere to the older practices quite literally, or, if they do not, feel guilty for not doing so. And there are the more progressive ones who have simply dropped many of the sustaining practices of the past — sometimes for good reasons — but who have replaced them with little or nothing in the way of a discipline or practice. There is little sign of exterior observance: they do not celebrate or attend Mass daily; they do not recite the breviary; they are seldom seen in the chapel or in an attitude of prayer. If they read the Bible daily or on a weekly basis there is little outward evidence of this. More importantly, there is little left in their lives of

[3] "The Future of Religious Life," in *Supplement to Doctrine and Life*, Dublin, Dominican Publications, May, 1972.

the bite of poverty or obedience. Admittedly they are hard-workers; if they are also priests, they will celebrate liturgy as often as some community desires it. They are often kind and thoughtful. They are often filled with apostolic fervor. But there is something missing. One type of spirituality, in its concrete aspects, has been set aside, and nothing has replaced it. Their religious life has no face. It does not give clear evidence of being a way of the vows, a way of worship and praise of the Lord in and through mortification and sacrifice. It is no longer a form of life which throws the life of Christ into literal and dramatic relief in the world. It is a religious life devoid of *elan* partly because it lacks a distinctive and concrete embodiment.

Some will answer: thank God, the beast is dead. Speaking as members of active apostolic religious congregations, they will say that they have legitimately shed a monastic spirituality which is no longer adequate for a modern apostolic congregation or for a world come of age. And yet, once again, what form of life has replaced it? It is the heresy of angelism to expect people to live a charism without providing a concrete embodiment of it. In what manner is this new form of religious existence an alternative lifestyle to that of the lay world? The new spirituality of which Rahner speaks must be not simply a slogan or a virtue or even only a charism or spirit, it must also be a form of life, a basic set of symbols and practices relating to the sacred, an asceticism and a discipline of prayer.

Sister Madeleine, a recently deceased Carmelite, stressed that the vows cannot remain mere attitudes, but must be concrete embodiments of a radical and worshipful stance toward God and of a love and service toward people. She says: "We know that the Church would not lose anything which is necessary for its basic structure and constitution if religious life did not exist. What it would lose is something that makes its life and holiness rich and radiant. It would lose the presence in it of those, who as Augustine says, 'live in their flesh what the whole Church lives by faith,' and that is the surpassing worth of knowing Jesus Christ and of living now his relationship to the Father as the one thing necessary."[4] Is not religious life designed to live out in some tangible and even literal sense, "in the flesh," the distinction between the Father and the world? In our valiant effort to be incarnational and identify closely with the laity, have we not perhaps lost sight of the mystical eschatological aspects of our vocation? Or is there a way of preserving these elements within the framework of a thorough-going incarnationalism? One thought keeps recurring: Without living a life which re-enacts the life and passion of Christ, religious will have little of depth to offer to the world.

Sister Madeleine recognizes that the vows are not primarily acts of renunciation. They are acts of worship which entail renunciation. But she goes on to stress that we have also to dutifully live out the negative side of our vocation. "There is . . . a paradox in our lives in that we are called to a certain emptiness for the sake of a God-given fullness. The emptiness entails willingly embracing the negations embraced in our state of life, not ignoring them, denying them, circumventing them with compensations, compromises, downright contradictions like a rich poverty, a self-willed obedience, an unchaste celibacy."[5] Here she is merely urging us to remember that religious life, though not superior to lay life, is an alternative way that, if it is to be authentic, must be a way of the Cross.

An analogy may be drawn between what has happened in religious life and the more general secularization of Western culture. With Bonhoeffer and Kierkegaard many thinkers called for a nonreligious Christianity, a Christianity cleared of all elements of the sacred, devoid of sacred times, places, persons, myths and rites. On this view the sacred is precisely what was overcome by Christ and the Gospel. Christianity was not another religion, but a faith. "Christendom must die, in order that Christianity might live" they chanted with Kierkegaard.

[4] "Religious Vows," *Religious Life Review*, March 1986, vol. 25, p. 63.

[5] *Ibid.*, p. 65.

Today, however, we realize that the sacred expressed in terms of myth, symbol, prayer, and ritual is a dimension of consciousness itself. To speak of discarding it is a practical contradiction. Jean Danielou, resisting radical secularization, spoke instead of the necessity of always retaining a "Christendom," a set of social structures which are bearers of the sacred. He called for a politics which fosters structures of prayer (*conditions de l'oraison*) at the heart of technical civilization. He insisted, however, that there was a correlative obligation on the part of Christianity not to simply continue in existence as a sociological residue of the past. It must rather come to grips with modern civilization. Christianity must foster a respect of the human person, struggle for the improvement of the condition of women and minorities, and for brotherhood among peoples of all races, even if the most important feature of Christianity will always be "the Incarnation of the Word and His Resurrection, the outpouring of the Spirit and the mission of the apostles, the conversion and the sanctification of hearts."[6]

[6] J. Danielou, *L'Oraison, probleme politique*, Fayard, 1965, p. 13.

There is a lesson here for religious life. It is not a desacralization that is needed but a purification of the sacred, a replacement of certain approaches to the sacred with an approach which truly confronts the challenge of modernity. Needed within our congregations is the creation of new "conditions of prayer," structures of personal and communal prayer and worship which serve to bring the Gospel to life in the membership and foster the constant conversion and sanctification of their hearts — structures that while directing them outward to the mission, also remind them that the center of religious life is the Incarnation and the Resurrection of the Lord.

If and when the need for a restructuring is accepted, then the difficult task begins. Which structures? What concrete forms of life will express the meaning of the vows for today? What forms of prayer will truly nourish the modern aspirant to religious life? Is there anything to be learned from the styles of prayer in other modern spiritual

45

movements? Have we thrown aside structures put in place by our founders in too cavalier a fashion? Have they not something to teach us about the very spirit and charism of the founder as I have intimated in the introduction to this book?

In such difficult matters no one can claim to have all the answers; we are still looking for the right questions. It is my conviction, however, that the road to the answer does not lie so much in ideas and theories but in flesh and blood persons. I allude here especially to the founder(s) of the congregation and to the saints in its history.

Father Raymond Hostie analyzes the similarities that existed historically in those exceptional congregations that, following a decline, did not die but were regenerated. The process of regeneration follows a pattern. Superiors are often the first to become alarmed. They spur and goad as well as they can. They multiply letters, visits and changes of personnel. But none of these efforts on the part of sheer authority seem to have any lasting effect. They succeed only in temporarily stemming the tide. "Every lasting reform," says Hostie, "is rooted in the phenomenon of a smallish group which takes up again on its own account the way of the foundation."[7] There is always a limited group within such congregations who again become fired with the spirit of the founder and try to restructure the congregation in line with this spirit. Some attempt to return literally to pristine practices, but the most successful are those like Teresa of Avila and John of the Cross, who reject a mere cult of the past and strive creatively for a true refoundation. Here the return to the sources is accompanied with spectacular and thoroughly unexpected innovations. These small groups have always been characterized also by doggedness; they reject squarely all half-measures in their effort to carry the pristine spirit into the present. So fierce is their wholeheartedness at times that, as in the case of the Capuchins *vis-a-vis* the Franciscans, they have been ejected, but not without

[7] Raymond Hostie, S.J., *La vie et la mort des ordres religieux*, p. 316.

46

enriching the Church with a new order and regenerating an older one.

Will not regeneration today again depend on a congregation being galvanized not by superiors, but by a small group of its members? A group which begins once again living out the primitive radicality according to a new set of practices and policies, living it out doggedly despite what anyone else does? A group which insists that the congregation divest itself of excess baggage in line with the spirit of poverty of the founder, a group whose members are willing to commit themselves to a larger cause and give priority to this cause over their own fulfillment, a group free enough to champion a re-evaluation of apostolates in an effort to give up those which are not in line with the inspiration of the founder, a group intent upon taking up a form of life which is redolent of the Gospel through and through? And all of this doggedly?

It is most essential for its continuation in the Church that the religious life be experienced as making a difference. It must be seen as making a difference in the line of sanctity. There must be present within it persons who are truly men and women of the Gospel, men and women whose primary goal is a personal union with the Lord. "I just want to love Him more and serve Him better," a religious sister said to me recently. They must not simply be people who are actively doing good. Like the apostles they must be people sent. With Jeremiah they must give forth the message that the name of God is like "a fire burning in my heart and imprisoned in my bones: I grow weary of holding it, I can no longer endure it." If religious life is not a fire it is nothing.

Only this will once again attract the young. There is as much idealism in today's world as there ever was. There is no less willingness to sacrifice and take on commitments. The difference is that, more than ever educated moderns ask for a reason — a reason verifiable in experience. "What difference will it make?" they ask. Nietzsche said and

Viktor Frankl was fond of repeating: "We can suffer any 'how' as long as we have a 'why'." The 'why' is what is missing today: why the sacrifice? As J.M.R. Tillard has said, the deeper aspect of the crisis of religious life is tied to the general crisis of the Church, the crisis of faith.

In principle such a crisis can be answered through reasoning but today it is often best answered existentially in living out a life which embraces the way of emptiness for the sake of the Lord, yet blossoms in human flourishing — a life in which one dies and yet rises again, in a special quality of presence, in fraternal love, and in the power of prophecy. In the eyes of today's culture the warrant of truth is meaningfulness. Epistemologically, it may not be the ultimate warrant, but if we are to gain a hearing it is there that we must begin.

Only the lure of the Gospel and the call of our founders will once again draw the young. Many of them are hungry for something which puts a question to the secular world which they inhabit and of which they to a great degree have had their fill. They long once again for visions, poetry and dreams. They are drawn to the Gospel and to a more literal re-enactment of the life of Christ. They desire to go with Him to a place apart. They are not afraid of His Cross, for they suspect that in the end His yoke may be easy and His burden light. They seek only a community of persons who have walked before them and know how to accompany them along the way.

4. CELIBACY, CATHEDRALS AND MODERN PSYCHOLOGY

The Cathedral of the Assumption in Mexico City sits astride the Zocalo, the spacious square surrounded by the buildings that form the seat of the Mexican government. As I stepped through the portals of the cathedral, my eyes were captured in the upward sweep of the columns toward the vaulted ceiling high above. As I stared in wonder at its sublimity I was overwhelmed by a sense of insignificance and, strangely, the thought came to mind that cathedrals and celibacy have much in common. Suddenly, for no special reason, I found myself thinking that if celibate chastity is problematic today, if it seems to many an unthinkable choice as well as the greatest deterrent to priestly and religious vocations, it is primarily because we have moved out of the world of cathedrals, a world in which constructing great sacred spaces seemed to make sense.

At the present time, both cathedrals and consecrated celibacy are under fire. Though people are amazed by the beauty and grandeur of these great churches, they would hardly agree to build one today, and sometimes ask why they were built in the past when the money could have been given to the poor. Pope John Paul II himself hesitated in the face of public opinion before consecrating the mammoth African cathedral in Ivory Coast. In similar fashion, some question why the Church imposes the rigor of celibacy on priests. Even some Catholic theologians challenge the celibacy rule and advance arguments in favor of a married clergy. Celibate chastity is at times viewed as a dysfunction, and a Church that imposes it as out of touch with the times. In the industrialized West it sometimes seems that only women want to become celibate priests.

If we prize celibate chastity less today, it is in part because we have forgotten the upward movement of religion toward God, of which the cathedral columns were a picture and a symbol. We have replaced it with a sideways thrust toward our brothers and sisters. Sacrifice, asceticism and mortification make sense only if they are relational, only if the sacrifice they demand results in easing the life of others in this vale of tears. We tend to disvalue piety and a life centered on a personal love-relationship with God in prayer and sacrament. Such piety is old-fashioned, quietistic, and built on overly romantic metaphors of a spiritual life lived in intimacy with God. We downplay the God of the desert in favor of building up the Kingdom in the marketplace.

Modernity can well be defined as the age of the flattening of the sacred, the collapsing of the distinction between the sacred and the profane. Evolutionary thinking has subtly invaded everywhere. In the modern mind, the subconscious picture of being contains only a material world in flux. It is the picture of one process of matter changing and structures arising within it, by accident or chance. There is little sense of any Being standing outside or above this process, no creative Logos or invisible divine hand within it. If there is a god, it is the world itself. As moderns we incline toward a cryptic pantheism.

And yet the Old Testament is filled with a sense of the mystical intimacy, involvement, and tender love of a God who is a person and transcends the world. The psalmist's lines overflow with yearning for the Lord, with wonder at His absence and gratitude for His presence. So Psalm 42:

> As a doe longs
> for running waters

> so longs my soul
>   for you my God.
>
> My soul thirsts for God,
>   for the God of life;
> when shall I go to see
>   the face of God?

The emphasis is on the relationship between creature and
Creator, on the deep thirst of the human heart. Despite a
thousand worldly involvements the psalmist craves the
height and the depth of the transcendent here symbolized
as living water.

    I don't know whether diocesan priests will one day
be allowed to marry. It could happen for, though the
prohibition dates back to the earliest centuries, some
theologians feel that it is a matter of Church law rather than
an immutable part of Christ's essential legacy. But the
matter must not be decided on the basis of some modern
bias or ideology. There are good arguments on both sides
of the issue and time must be taken in coming to a
conclusion. Theologians are reflecting on the matter and
will advise the Church, and the Pope and bishops will
ultimately decide. But the question of mandatory priestly
celibacy is not at issue in this writing. Celibate chastity, the
voluntary and lifelong renunciation of all genital sexual
acts, is an essential element for religious life and remains, I
believe, a very important symbol for priestly existence.
One thing, at least, is clear, that our response to the signs
of the times need not always take the form of capitulating
to the times by taking the easier path. While we must learn
to listen for Gospel voices present within the modern world
and its trends, we must also discern its corrosive elements
and not fear to be counter-cultural.

    In this essay, I will limit myself to discussing the
meaning of celibate chastity and why it should be retained
in some form as an important Christian practice in the
Church. In the process I will also discuss some reasons why

contemporary psychology has made it problematic.

The columns of the cathedral of Mexico City spoke an important word to me about the link between celibate chastity and the love of God. As I followed their flight into the architectural heaven of the cathedral, I was seized by the thought that no matter how beautiful was erotic passion — the intertwining of bodies and the exchange of carnal joy — there was something even more sublime. There was something more beautiful than even the wonderful love that transports two persons into an enchanted circle and makes them feel that they are alive for the first time.

A phrase resounded in my mind as if spoken by some inner voice: "Celibacy is the symbol of a life that towers into the holy." So powerful was the thought that it put me in mind of the voices that used to speak to Joan of Arc. It was as if the upward thrust of the columns was reminding me that while we can walk as Christians we can also soar. It brought me face to face with the transcendent dimension of which celibate chastity has always been a pointer and a sign. The phrase remained with me for days and subtly changed me. It expelled from my heart a worm of doubt about religious life and the vow of chastity that had gnawed for several years. Like a light in the darkness it brought a quiet strength. It reminded me of something from which we have been distracted: that beyond all human interactions — with plants and animals, with minerals and machines, with other human beings, there is another possibility of intercourse and conversation — with the living God.

Belief in God expands our world. It reveals that a zone of mystery surrounds ordinary life. We now see our life as set within an enchanted region and a mystical space, within the holy dimension of a God of love who inspires not abject fear and terror, but quiet awe and wonder. If the Church has done anything down the years, it has succeeded in preserving the message that there is eternity in time, and that for this reason, the world is not absurd or devoid of meaning.

What is the reason for the crisis of celibate chastity in today's Church? The root reason is the levelling of dimensions. Michael Buckley, S.J. has said that American atheism is rooted in the conviction that empirical science and its methodology is the sole road to knowledge in all fields of investigation, not only in the fields of physics and biology, but even when dealing with questions about God or morality. Science extending itself beyond its brief has become the new metaphysics. We have become "one-dimensional" men and women whose thought is reductive and unimaginative.

The crisis of celibacy and chastity is allied to the death of grand causes, of great adventures that reach beyond time to eternity. "The world is too much with us," said Wordsworth in another context, "getting and spending we lay waste our powers." In our distrust of our powers to transcend the world, we cling insecurely to the world. In an overly secularized religiosity we stress a Christianity that pays off and pays off now. We repeat such phrases as "salvation begins on earth" and the words of Irenaeus that "the glory of God is man fully alive." But I wonder what is the deep meaning of these currents. Are we legitimately trying to correct the exaggerations of an otherworldly spirituality, or do we, in our heart of hearts, not quite believe in a life after death, in an eternal life with God? Are we in danger of being caught in another time-bound humanism? Yet, if Christianity is not for eternity, can it have any meaning even for now?

Many dislike distinctions between the transcendent and the world, the sacred and the profane. They fear that talk about the "sacred" will siphon off the value of the world. For this reason many modern thinkers canonize sinners, and say there is little difference between virgins and prostitutes, that saints and thieves are the same, that we are all in the world as "passengers without tickets" (Sartre).

But if nothing is holy it is difficult to find a ground for the dignity of human beings. The Biblical ground for

human dignity lies in the fact that God created us even
though He had no need for us. He created us out of sheer
love. Atheists, of course, resist this way of grounding the
dignity of the human person. They try, instead, to root it in
the fact that of all creatures, humans alone possess
freedom, the ability to choose between values and to
decide how they will act. It is because they have freedom
and philosophically are self-starters, said Kant, that human
beings do not have a price, but a dignity. And he went on
to interpret the symbols and dogmas of Christianity as mere
goads to leading a Kantian moral life.

But the attempt to ground human dignity upon
human freedom, characteristic of the Enlightenment, has
clearly failed. Scientists themselves have become sorely
aware of the limits of science and of a philosophy built on
an overconfidence in science. For this reason the most
recent skeptical philosophers, the deconstructionists, have
taken another tack. They begin by granting that the idea of
human dignity is essentially tied to belief in a loving
Creator and divine Lawgiver. But because they cannot
believe in such a God, they simply discard the whole idea
of human dignity. They bite the bullet and admit that
human life has no deep meaning, and human beings no
special standing in the universe. Some go even further and
urge that the whole truth game be discarded, because there
is no objective truth. All systems — natural science, art,
morality and religion — are games which humans concoct
to serve arbitrary purposes and ultimately to distract
themselves from the heart of darkness. American
philosopher Richard Rorty, for example, recently declared
his staunch support for the system of Western democracy,
but also admits that there is no way of rationally grounding
his preference. The only way he can think of staving off
critics of current democratic practices is by declaring them
fanatics who are out of step with the times. As examples of
fanatics he cites the philosopher Nietzsche and St. Ignatius
of Loyola.

Just as the notion of human dignity falls without

belief in a transcendent God, so too celibate chastity seems absurd unless our life is once again trained on God and His glory, unless we once again fashion for modern times an area of sacred space, sacred time, and sacred persons — unless we rediscover and remake, in a modern way, the world of cathedrals.

Note that even if celibate chastity has lost meaning for some Church persons, it continues to fascinate the world. It is the aspect of a priest or religious that makes the most concrete impact on them, for it opens up a world of surprise. After getting to know a priest or a religious for a while, young people never fail to ask: "Why can't you get married?" Celibacy intrigues people because it is out of the ordinary; it is a symbol of the Kingdom of God and its novelty. Again why is it that the failures of priests and religious in the area of sexual abuse makes prime-time news, even though the proportion of priest-offenders simply reflects that of the wider population? It may be due to the media's opposition to the Catholic Church's general stand on sexual modesty and marital fidelity. But I believe there is another reason. If failures of priests gain such attention, it is because people know that the role of the priest is to be a bridge to the transcendent. He alone enters the holy of holies and consecrates the bread and wine. If failures of religious gain so much attention, it is because by a public vow they have proclaimed themselves as standing in a special way with the Lord. Even those who believe that priests and religious are not called to a special degree of holiness, feel that they, more than others caught in sexual abuse, have betrayed a special trust.

The American Church and the bishops must be commended with the way they have responded to the pedophilia crisis. Perhaps they could do more, but in general they have faced the issue squarely. They agree that our central concern must be for past and potential victims and that offenders must be prosecuted and summarily removed from ministry, and are presently acting on this conviction. I believe it is quite unfair to blame the Church as an institution for the way it previously handled such cases. If its past practice was to treat it as a passing failure, to rehabilitate and reassign, as it did in other kinds of moral lapses, it was because at the time the defining characteristics of pedophilia were not well understood by anyone. Until very recently, neither the Church nor the behavioral sciences understood the compulsive and repetitive nature of the psychological defect of pedophilia, how much denial can be involved, and how it is more compulsive and fixated when the sexual attraction is toward young children (pedophilia) rather than toward adolescents (ephebophila). If we indict the Church for its past ignorance, we must also indict doctors, psychologists, lawyers and scientists for theirs. Now that the profile of the pedophile is more clearly defined, we can all take more adequate measures whether the problem appears in the ministry, in families, or in the social services.

Sexuality, a Basic Dimension

If one aspect of the crisis of celibate chastity stems from secularization and the loss of the sense of the sacred, another aspect arises from the side of psychology and philosophy. Early in this century Marxist thinkers trivialized sex by calling it a "drink of water." But most modern philosophers and psychologists disagree and view sexuality as a basic dimension of human existence. Sexuality is not something we engage in only from time to time. Our every thought and action has a sexual aspect; at every moment we are not only male and female, but masculine and feminine. The fact that we are attracted to others and seek sexual fulfillment through them, reveals that as humans we are not merely persons, but co-persons. The sexual side of our nature signals that we are not just atoms or individual subjects but are social beings from the very first moment.

It is precisely because sexuality is so fundamental, that some contend that no one should be constrained by law to renounce it. But on the other hand, if sexuality is so basic, then the renunciation of sexual activity becomes ever more important and is arguably one of the greatest gifts we can make to God. If sexuality is more central to our existence than our skin, setting aside its exercise is not the mere refusal of the Marxists' glass of water. It is a most apt symbol of an outright gift of our deepest self.

Sigmund Freud cannot be accused of considering sexuality trivial. It is he, in fact, who is at the genesis of the prevailing view that sexuality pervades our existence. Freud taught that all human conduct was motored by unconscious sexual desires which he called "libido" and that neuroses and psychoses were due to unresolved sexual conflict. The very slips of our tongue arose from repressed sexual desire and our most insignificant dreams were sexual wishes in masquerade. By carefully analyzing the masquerade we could discern the underlying sexual desires. Psychological problems occurred when we consciously suppressed or unconsciously repressed these wishes. The cure came from bringing unconscious sexual conflicts into consciousness and gaining insight into them. This process began with the help of a trained analyst, who would surface the unconscious material through deciphering our dreams and making sense of our free association of ideas. However, the real cure came through a process called transference, where the client transfers to the analyst much of the emotional charge surrounding his or her repressed desires and re-lives it in a more mature manner.

Freud's error lay in believing he could fashion a general theory of sexuality out of an insight that was valid for a particular epoch. Though the theory of sexual repression explained well symptoms apparent in Victorian society, it was soon seen to be inadequate as a general theory of human psychology. Jung and Adler, his pupils, distanced themselves from Freud's pansexualism and wisely construed human energy or libido as a more diversified force. Contemporary psychologists remain basically Freudian but temper his excesses. They are far more eclectic and pragmatic, applying different therapies to different problems. *Time* magazine recently carried major articles criticizing some aspects of Freudian theory as well as the reliance of courts of law on Freud's theory that people may completely repress painful memories and later recall them. The authors claim that overconfidence in this questionable theory has resulted in the conviction and imprisonment of the innocent.

Celibacy and Modern Psychology

Despite recent reaction against Freudian theory, especially in the area of the recovery of repressed memories, it cannot be denied that during the mid-20th century a whole ethos grew up around Freud's psychological revolution. The English language was literally invaded with Freudian metaphors, from the "Oedipus complex" to the "id," and from the "superego" to the "Freudian slip." This influence did not fail to penetrate the walls of convent and cloister. Perhaps because they tend to be more introspective than the general population, men and women in religious congregations as well as diocesan priests and Protestant ministers, took modern psychology extremely seriously and subconsciously turned Freudian concepts into a religion, at times swallowing his erroneous assumptions and exaggerations along with his insights.

It was especially in the 1950's and 1960's that the tenets of clinical psychology invaded the seminaries and religious novitiates and scholasticates. Psychological testing became mandatory and vocational screening was based on their results. The results of these tests were often considered overriding, despite the fact that clinical psychologists advised that they were less reliable than the daily observation of the seminary staff that lived in the same community as the seminarians.

Prior to the advent of modern psychology, seminary and novitiate staffs evaluated aspirants on the basis of totally different assumptions. They expressed their evaluation in terms of virtues and vices. They might, for example, label a certain candidate "lazy." This certainly imputed blame and perhaps caused guilt-feelings, but it also suggested that because the candidate was responsible for becoming lazy, he also had the freedom to change and become industrious. On the other hand, younger, more "enlightened" professors, like myself, preferred a psychological language which construed an aspirant's erratic behavior as arising from unfulfilled emotional needs. A particular candidate was not "lazy," he had a great need for "succorance" — to be mothered by others. Another's need was for "nurturance" — to show maternal care to others. Another had a need for "affiliation" — to have deep and emotional personal relationships, or for "heterosexuality," or for "homosexuality," etc.

We did not realize it at the time but we were viewing human action on the model of a parallelogram of conflicting forces, implying that because a person had certain needs he could not help but do what he did. In this way we were robbing them of a great measure of their freedom. We were sapping their ability to take responsibility for their lives and to change.

Even though it is much more nuanced, modern psychology is still a major influence in religious life. It has shifted away from Freudian to Jungian categories, and most religious can categorize you under one of the possible four-letter categories of the Myers-Briggs test. But it was within the Freudian days of the mid-20th century that it suddenly seemed certain to many that one could not attain emotional maturity without a meaningful interpersonal relationship with a person of the opposite sex. Many onlookers and some Church persons adopted the fashionable thesis that a chastity strictly adhered to was either impossible, or at the very least, psychologically unhealthy, leading to eccentricity and the stunting of personality.

The acceptance of Freudian ideas on the damaging

effect of repression produced, in society in general, a full-scale release of the sexual imagination. Everything was allowed at least at the level of fantasy. Guilt-feelings were no longer considered salutary pain-signals resulting from moral misuse of freedom, but were simply to be banished. "Bad thoughts" became the object of bad jokes. Oscar Wilde's advice that the best way to be rid of temptations was to give into them, suddenly did not seem so cynical. Monkish practices like "custody of the eyes" were deemed quaint and others like self-chastisement with a whip called "taking the discipline," were clearly masochistic. Like infants in Freud's theory, the monks of the past were "polymorphous perverts" taking the vow of chastity but giving vent to their sexuality in cute and naughty little ways.

It is clear that the Freudian revolution in sexual mores was and remains one of the major causes of the decline of priestly and religious vocations and of the exodus of priests and religious from their vowed obligations. Many believed that the world had entered a phase of sexual enlightenment which a reluctant Church would eventually come to embrace. So they left while they were still young enough. Some of those who stayed began to live a kind of double life. They spoke less and less of a "vow of chastity" which excluded all genital activity, and more of a "vow of celibacy" which explicitly excluded only the taking of a husband or wife. They began to experiment with new ways of "celibacy" which allowed some sexual expression, and which for a short time became known as the "third way." As long as you did not marry it seemed legitimate, and psychologically desirable, to date, to hold intimate conversation, and outwardly express your affection toward the other sex. Logically, it seemed to follow that a person of homosexual orientation possessed identical rights to the same degree of sexual expression. And so now we are where we are in religious life — a life of the divided heart; a collection of lifestyles built on a variety of loves.

In her book, *New Wineskins,* Sandra Schneiders

blames the apparent upsurge in sexual aberrations among priests and religious on a seminary or religious training that has left them sexually adolescent. However true, this is only part of the story. The first point to be made is that the percentage of priests and religious who fall into the sin of pedophilia is identical with the general population, even if the media, for various reasons, focuses attention on them. Second, in partial support of Schneiders' thesis, it is true that a prolonged separation from dealings with members of the opposite sex renders a celibate's picture of that sex idealistic and unreal. The overly-protected celibate tends to relate not to flesh and blood men and women but to men and women of fantasy. This is dangerous because the imagination deals in pictures, and pictures by necessity emphasize some aspects of a subject to the exclusion of others. Thus, fantasized sex can narrow the focus of the sexual urge to a particular aspect of a person while leaving aside many others. The imagination can become obsessed with a person's shape, muscular strength or sexy voice, and completely disregard other positive and negative features. On the other hand, real life experience is like a walk down a beach with its sobering mixture of beauty and cellulite. It corrects the imagination's narrowness by filling in the picture. It reveals that the perfect human form hardly ever exists outside the mind, and if it does, it can be accompanied by many other things, like a devious personality or a banal mind.

But the isolated training of an earlier seminary or convent is not the only source of the increase in aberrant sexual behavior. To contend that it is, is to turn a blind eye to the pervasive influence of a sex-crazed media, a media recently described by Cardinal Carlo Martini as an "atmosphere." Nor can liberal-leaning reformers of religious life and priesthood place all the blame on traditional training. If the last 30 years gives evidence of an increase in aberrant sexual fantasizing and acting-out in priests and religious, it is not because seminary authorities have tightened up seminary restrictions concerning modesty and relationships or because contemporary moral theology has preserved the rigidity of the past in matters sexual. Just the opposite is true: concomitant with the increase in sexual acting-out has been a move in the direction of greater tolerance, experimentation, and even permissiveness. In seminaries and convents, much that was formerly supported by community structures is now handled personally. The stress is on the needs of the individual. But since sexuality is such a potent force, must not the lines be clearly drawn? If they are blurred, is there not a danger that temptation will turn into invitation?

Priests and religious of past centuries, and even those of the early 20th century, experienced inclinations and temptations similar to those trained in more recent years. And yet they did not often translate these inclinations into action nor did they so easily set aside their vowed obligations. Why was this? Was it not in part due to their wise lack of confidence in a person's ability to go it alone, to their salutary dependency on structures and a common discipline? Was it not because they lived in a totally different cultural atmosphere when the shibboleths of a superficial freedom were not shouted into one's ears from all sides? Was it not due to a self-imposed discipline in which they had been trained? I once overheard an elderly priest being accused by a young religious of being in a rut because of his routine of life and prayer. He responded: "Yes, and it took me a long time to get into that rut. Without it I would have been lost." If sexual lapses of all kinds are occurring with greater frequency now, must not part of the blame be placed on the turn to self-expression and social experimentation?

Sexuality is a strong instinctual force whose expression must be controlled in every culture. At adolescence sexuality makes itself felt as a stranger in the house of the spirit. Especially in adolescent males, it arrives with dramatic intensity and at times may seem compulsive and unyielding. So it became clear to the Church that without safeguards and support from the example of others, without building will-power and being vigilant in prayer, all promises to be eunuchs for the Kingdom would be in vain. It is for this reason that sexuality was hedged about with rules and why religious founders often spoke of mutual support and edification. The need for such regulation and support becomes even more imperative in a culture wherein sexual tolerance is all-pervasive, invading advertising, movies, novels, and television and even courts of law.

The modern world teaches that nothing is valuable except pleasant states of consciousness. It teaches, furthermore, that the content of such states can vary widely from person to person, and for this reason the major moral right is freedom, and our principal social duty, tolerance. Any opposition to such a stance is met with the retort that tolerance is better than fascism. True, but if this is all that can be said in its favor, it is like saying that America is great because it is not like Rwanda.

The major objection to the primacy of tolerance, is that it impoverishes society by eviscerating the importance of other values, the very values that give substance to our life and help us build families and other associations. It de-emphasizes virtues like courage and temperance which demand discipline and self-sacrifice. It subtly attacks the family by suggesting to parents that more important than the care of children is the quality of one's own life. It has led to a vaunting increase in divorce on the now discredited plea that the children of the divorced would do just fine.

Modern permissiveness in matters sexual seems to offer freedom, but it actually constricts our choices and enslaves us. It urges us to submit because, in the last analysis, we cannot do otherwise. It claims that temptations will not subside unless we surrender to them. For all its talk of freedom, it really believes that we are not free at all and that our behavior is prisoner to our biological tendencies or to our culture. On the other hand, the traditional philosophy of sexual restraint and self-control, is convinced of our ability to choose between submitting and exercising a strong control over our lives, and knows that through a repetition of acts of self-control, our freedom will grow and develop.

At times sexuality can seem totally compulsive and uncontrollable. It seems to borrow an inner voice that says: "this must be." We all recognize the feeling. And yet we also know from experience that there is another inner voice to be borrowed. It is a voice which says: "You really don't need this to be happy." And if we pause to heed it, there is often a change of mood, and we sense that it is possible to gently put aside that which just a moment before seemed so intractable. This second voice is the voice of our freedom, that part of us that opens out to ever new possibilities and assures us that we are not caught in a narrow cage. It breaks the spell of the sexual urge that tends to contract possibilities and make us, as women often complain, "think of only one thing."

I am convinced of the value of celibate chastity and that it must be retained in the Church, at least as part of any renewed form of religious life. Celibate chastity, moreover, is valuable in itself and not merely on pragmatic grounds or because of some instrumental value. It is not to be prized primarily because, by disencumbering us of interpersonal tangles or family obligations, it frees us to use our time doing good for others. Free time, after all, is a relative concept, and does not always translate into greater industry. "If you want something done," says the proverb, "ask the busy man." Neither is celibacy's importance based primarily on its witness value, on its power to lead others to prefer God over worldly creatures and concerns. Celibate chastity is not valuable primarily for what it frees us from nor in being a sign for others. It is intrinsically valuable in itself, because it is a special way of being with God.

Celibate chastity is the erotic love of God. Far from being sexless, it is a love of God expressed not thinly by the mind and will, but thickly, through the body. It is a dramatic reminder for all the people of God, signaled through the gift of the bodies of some of its members, that union with God is "a song which does not die in the hearing, a flavor which does not abate in the eating, an embrace which gives delight without end" (St. Augustine). Celibate chastity is one particular way of answering the call to holiness issued to all of us in baptism. It is important because sex is important. Taking this vow, a person announces to God that more important than the beautiful love which can exist between a man and woman, is the surpassing love of Jesus Christ our Lord and God. In pronouncing this vow, we are not only offering ourselves for service to the world nor only witnessing to others, but doing, in Mother Teresa's words, "something beautiful for God."

After Freud

At long last the love-affair with Freud and his followers is ending. Psychologists are discovering that though Freud's ideas may have accurately described the problems of Viennese culture of the late 19th century, their value as a general theory of psychology is limited. They have realized that sexual repression cannot be a major cause of contemporary psychological problems, mainly because such repression no longer exists. In fact, our problems may be due to an over-expression of sexuality, the use of sex to cope with frustration, at times called "panic sex." Today most psychological problems spring from meaninglessness, the sense that life in a consumer society is hollow, that all is banal and trivial. Depression, not repression, is the illness of the baby-boomers. The vacuum of meaning foments anxiety and the response is often an escape into the reverie of drugs or to kinky expressions of a jaded sexuality.

Paradoxically, celibate chastity and its atmosphere of restraint can help the world regain the "sexiness" of sexual experience. Without a due asceticism, pleasures become less pleasurable. This is a lesson of which the Epicureans —the old pleasure experts — were acutely aware, and which we neo-Epicureans seem to have forgotten. Ermanno Olmi's lovely film, *The Tree of the Wooden Clogs*, brought it home to me. In the atmosphere of cultural restraint and courtesy in which the story is set, the mere "good evening" of a youth furtively whispered to a lass in the twilight, becomes an erotic transaction.

Modern psychology has valuable insights and can provide relief to many people when used wisely. It helps to untie knots and complications. It has shown, for instance, that sexual difficulties can manifest and mask other difficulties. Some people turn to sex as a substitute for anger, others in order to relieve frustration, others to cover over a need to dominate. Through such insights we become aware of the intricacy of our inner life, and are freer to deal maturely with our behavior.

Reference to competent psychologists is also imperative when one suspects certain gross aberrations like schizophrenia. Psychology is most reliable and more truly scientific in respect to such gross ailments because, as is now widely admitted, they have a biological or physical base and their symptoms are thus more recurrent and less variant. In this way psychology had been able to develop an adequate classification of aberrations like schizophrenia and paranoia and has been able to define them in terms of certain hard and fast symptoms. For instance, one of the classical signs of schizophrenia is a patient's belief that ideas are being inserted into his mind by some outside force. In the absence of such classical symptoms the ailment is not schizophrenia, but something else. Such knowledge is extremely valuable and prevents us from making gross mistakes.

Another positive development is that psychologists have become less arrogant and have, for the most part, given up sallies into philosophy and theology. Remaining within their own competence, they no longer try to explain away religion and morality. They have also become more eclectic and do not accept the rigid assumptions of one or other psychological school. Different approaches from different schools are adopted on a pragmatic basis, on the grounds of what works. Thus behavior-modification techniques might be mixed with Freudian psychoanalysis and such extreme measures as electro-shock therapy might be used to counter serious depressions. Instead of the long therapy of psychoanalysis, anti-depressants like Prozac are prescribed for obsessive-compulsive disorder, the need to endlessly repeat irrational acts like washing one's hands a hundred times a day. A contemporary psychologist is generally less ideological and doctrinaire than those of an earlier generation and more pragmatic and flexible.

In a general way, psychology has been admirable in aiding people to be aware of their feelings, to become more supple, less rigid, and to be able in a sense to walk around within themselves and to discover the hidden corners of their soul. As employed in programs modelled on Clinical Pastoral Education, it has enriched ministry by initiating a type of training that makes connections between the head and the heart, between the intellect and the emotions. It has helped us to deal more frankly and openly with each other and taught us the skills of a fraternal confrontation. It has aided many to rise out of dysfunctional dependency to a healthy autonomy, to an ability to trust and to forgive themselves as well as others, and to make the move to a true interdependence in a common cause.

But in its effect on religious life contemporary psychology has also had its shadow-side, especially where it has led to excessive self-involvement. The repeated self-analysis of some priests and religious can at times appear excessive and even morbid. Worse than this, often it has not seemed to do them much good. Their self-absorption brings to mind Wittgenstein's image of the philosopher, whom he compares to "a fly in a fly-bottle." Not aware that the bottle is open, the fly struggles frantically and beats repeatedly against the glass. I sometimes think that more would be gained if a person gave up the effort to discover himself by means of an inner trip, and replaced it with an outer one. I wonder whether it would not be better if one resisted the temptation to self-examination, so often filled with self-pity, and turned one's thoughts to the needs of others. I suggest this not as a means of avoidance but as a possible way of releasing deeper energies and more effectively developing the sorely sought sense of self-esteem. To be even more dramatic, might there not even be some value in a degree of old-fashioned repression? Can we have come to a point of over-analysis and over-communication? Might it not be healthier to reserve a silent room within one's soul, where the impulse to analyze is quietly put aside, and the desire to "share" gently declined?

One clinical psychologist who specialized in problems of homosexuality told a group of religious that in his experience the best answer to loneliness for a religious of homosexual orientation was long hours spent communing with the Lord present in the Eucharist. It was there that many were finding the loyal faithful friend of their deepest longing. Despite the Catholic-bashing of much of the media, we must not be blind to the great wisdom present in the Church's system of sacraments and sacramentals. We should also recognize that the *cura animarum* has as much to learn from the experience of the Fathers of the Church and the lives of the saints as from a psychology which is still in its infancy and whose assumptions and basic values are at times suspect.

The principal rationale for the life of religious is to be in intimate contact with the Lord and by their life to symbolize to others a dimension of existence that transcends the human. While extolling what is valuable in the world in the spirit of *Gaudium et Spes*, they must also urge their contemporaries to step beyond the world and its humanistic solutions. Their task is to build a bridge to the sacred. They do this by themselves entering upon a religious journey together — the journey of John the Baptist, who because he went into the desert, was credible when he came forth to declare: "He must increase and I must decrease." They must proclaim to the world the words of Jesus to the Samaritan woman: "If you but knew the gift of God!" Celibate chastity may not be an absolutely necessary requirement for those charged with this role, but, as I learned in Mexico's beautiful cathedral, it is a very apt symbol.

5. FAITH AND JUSTICE:
A DELICATE BALANCE

As I have already intimated in Chapters One and Two, a common feature of contemporary theologies has been the tendency to transform religion into social ethics, politics or even ecology. In this chapter we will try to examine this phenomenon more closely as it affects contemporary religious life.

Many modern theologians present the Christian religion as bearing less on how we relate to God and more on how we treat other human beings. This tendency was dramatically present in the "death of God" theologies of the 1960's, but is apparent as well in the work of some German and Dutch Catholic theologians, in the theology of hope, in feminist and black theology, in the theology of liberation, and most recently in certain creation theologies that highlight ecology. These newer theologies spur the construction of a world of freedom, equality and justice and they criticize classical theology for its otherworldliness and its social elitism.

Much of this is borrowed directly from Marx, whose thought is rooted in the Enlightenment and its secularizing tendencies. His critique of religion as a passing epiphenomenon, ultimately flawed as recent events in Eastern Europe have shown, has, however, been salutary. Its sting has been partly responsible for the Church's modern focus on a preferential option for the poor. Its atheism and excesses apart, we must thank Marxism for helping to bring the Church down to earth, for re-igniting incarnational theology, for toning down a naive type of eschatology and for highlighting systemic and institutional evil. It must also be admitted, on the other hand, that its influence within Christianity has not been totally beneficial. Some within the Church, especially some members of religious congregations, may have embraced somewhat uncritically some of Marx's more questionable attitudes and viewpoints. It is important for the future of religious life in the Church that the negative as well as the positive aspects of the turn to peace and justice be examined and evaluated.

Theologian J.M.R. Tillard, O.P., complains that some religious dedicated to peace and justice, those who consider the task of transforming the human as central to Christianity, seem thoroughly seduced by the ideal of the earthly kingdom.[1] Social change, human rights, equality of opportunity and the eradication of poverty not only are important to them, but are their consuming interest.

It may be a hard saying, but it seems to me that some peace and justice workers, in a way similar to Marx, have lost sight of the deep meaning of Christianity as well as confidence in the Resurrection. Partly due to a lack of faith in otherworldly and eschatological realities, they have found it necessary to find a totally earthly locus for their passion. As I indicated above (Chapter One) they continue to use God-language and to quote the Scriptures, but on their lips such language often seems a mythic overlay, a symbolic vehicle for motivating people to become engaged in the more important task of social, economic, and ecological reform.

They speak frequently of the need to "build up the Kingdom" and insist that "salvation must begin on earth" but have only lip-service for the eschatological aspects of the Kingdom and salvation. They are more at home with social action and politics than with piety, with prayer of petition, with praise of the Lord. They espouse most of the liberal or radical social causes of the day, criticizing neo-conservatism as escapism and remain quite silent on moral issues such as abortion. They tend to shy away from the

[1] *Dans le monde, pas du monde,* Brussels, Lumen Vitae, 1981, p. 17.

"mere sacramental ministry" and at times translate liturgy into a political statement. They downplay mortification which is merely ascetical and has no connection with relieving the lot of the poor. At times they seem not to examine sufficiently the implications of the type of freedom and tolerance that contemporary democracy espouses. Some do not seem sufficiently aware that, as theologian Gerald Collins, S.J., reminds us, for Christians, the Kingdom does not come *from* history but must be *given to* history. An unbalanced interpretation of the Incarnation has led to a kind of reductionism and at times even to a cryptic atheism.

Lest this interpretation seem too severe, I hasten to add that I criticize the form that social involvement has taken for some in the Church with great reluctance. First of all, it is clear that in the history of the Church priests, monks and sisters have been involved in all types of work in behalf of the poor. Practically no area of ministry was off-limits to religious and reserved for the laity. Monks, sisters and priests dedicated their lives for the ransom of captives, they ran inns and hostels, helped build towns, and taught trades to primitive peoples. The "following of Christ" (*sequela Christi*) does not refer only to the seeking the *other world* which will come into being on the last day when Christ delivers the Kingdom to the Father (1 Cor 15:24-28). It refers also to this world which is destined to be a changed world, or in the words of Tillard, "a *world made other*, a world where humanity will appear as God destined it to be, sustained in peace, justice and mutual love."[2] The new theology of religious life has displaced the strong hierarchy of goals in the mission of religious congregations, which once gave primacy to the striving for personal holiness over ministry to the neighbor.

Secondly, I concur strongly with the words of Pope John Paul II writing to the bishops of Brazil on April 9, 1986, that as an extension of classical theology, some form of liberation theology is necessary. In no way do I desire to provide priests and religious with lame excuses for

[2] *Dilemmas of Modern Religious Life*, Wilmington, Delaware, Michael Glazier, 1984, p. 15.

avoiding questions of social justice. In the contemporary world, where advances in social analysis and communication make us keenly aware of gross injustices, involvement in peace and justice ministries may be the acid test of true Christian faith. At times, direct involvement by religious in political action may be required.

Furthermore, in my own visits to Peru, Brazil, Mexico, and the Philippines, I have come into contact with peoples and lands ravaged by the corruption of political leaders and the rapacious greed of multi-national corporations. I have shivered at the burials of infants who died because their parents lacked the rudimentary education needed to assure them simple hygienic or medical care. I have endured the odors of the "*cortiçoes*" of Sao Paolo, where entire families live in the cramped squalor of a single room. I have been moved by the books of Gutierrez, Sobrino, and other liberation theologians, as well as by the reflections of Thomas E. Clarke, S.J., on the deep theological meaning of the option for the poor.[3] With Father Clarke, I too desire that the Church be transformed into a community of *anawim* — the biblical term for the lowly poor who put their trust in God — for the blessing of the world.

[3] Thomas E. Clarke, S.J., "Option for the Poor: A Reflection," *America*, January 30, 1988.

In October 1991 Pope John Paul II visited Brazil. The scenes of the visit were especially stirring. As is usual in these papal visits, most moving was his encounter with young people. Gathered around him in Salvador, the capital of the impoverished northern region of Bahia, were 30,000 children. As he spoke, the children were overcome with emotion and tears streamed down their cheeks. He said that the world would not be civilized until children were happy, until they were all smiling and frolicking. It must stop using them for profit in pornography, prostitution and drug-dealing. It must make sure that all had sufficient food and no longer needed to prowl the streets like bands of wolves. Children must no longer be sequestered in reformatories that do not re-train but merely teach them new vices before releasing them into the back alleys of Sao Paulo.

Poverty also exists in the United States, but on a scale totally different from that found in parts of Brazil, in Bangladesh and the Philippines. America cannot be truly great unless it does something about the world's dire poor, unless it champions their cause before the family of nations. In this area ours are sins of omission. We take a look and are revulsed by what we see, and then we avert our eyes, we distract ourselves and change the subject.

It is mainly because they do have a deep concern for the poorest and the marginalized that religious have rushed headlong into social work, and consider as central the task of transforming the world in terms of remedying poverty and restoring human dignity, at a time when the resources of the world for the first time seem adequate to achieve such a task. When one is personally touched by people suffering and sees in their eyes the desire for immediate relief, all else becomes idle theory. When you have seen an entire family living in one miserable room, how can you feel comfortable owning a whole house?

As a result, whole groups of religious have taken up residence in *favelas* to be with the poor, to share and better their lot. Their intentions have been admirable and their courage, compassion, and zeal beyond question. But as in all ventures, great and small, there has been a shadow-side. Some became radical and espoused now outmoded Marxist theories of class struggle requiring confrontation and violence. Those who avoided violence still seemed yoked to an ideological form of structural analysis which caused them to overstress the political aspects of Christianity. A number saw their own vocations founder because they tried to share the social life of people in all its aspects, staying up late into the night to eat and drink with the people, to celebrate and mourn with them. Overly tired, they found themselves neglecting prayer, recollection in solitude, and common spiritual practices. A significant number eventually left their congregations on the plea that the "spiritual" side of their commitment was dated and no longer relevant. Fostering a personal union with God was simply too individualistic; it distracted from the principal task of social reform. Yet without this primary source of strength they became spiritually "burnt out" and were lost to the cause of social justice itself, a phenomenon concerning which even secular journals like *U.S. News & World Report* sadly took note.

It is precisely because the Church's social endeavor is so important that it is in danger of becoming an idol. Because its aim is to improve the worldly lot of the oppressed, those engaged in it can easily succumb to the temptation of secularism. Because it is focused so squarely upon transforming the lot of the other, it can cause us to lose sight of the Wholly Other.

Truly effective social work must have a religious center. It must be rooted in an affirmation of God, be centered on the Gospel, and emanate from a deep life of prayer. It must be rooted in a spirituality that not only sustains the worker but also provides a ground for true social concern.

In preaching care for the poor and identity with them, we must beware of the ever-present temptation of reducing humanity to its mere economic or political dimensions to the exclusion of the religious one. Politics deals primarily with our relationship to one another. Religion is concerned primarily with our relationship to God. The primary vocation of every Christian, rich or poor, is to adore and thank the Lord and celebrate the glory of God. The poor themselves are keenly aware of this. They, too, are made for the infinite and the everlasting. They too pine for God as does the deer for running waters. Their hearts, like ours, are restless until they rest in the Lord.

To go to the poor solely with the promise of justice, or with dynamics aimed at helping them bring about structural or agrarian reform is to underrate them. This does not mean that in working with them we must limit ourselves to considerations about contemplative prayer or the Beatific Vision. It does mean that we cannot remain at the level of material betterment and emotional support. We must go to them with a greater gift. More than this, we must go to them to ourselves receive this greater gift. Because they are the chosen ones of the Lord, it is through them, first and foremost, that we learn who the Lord is.

Marxism and other mere humanisms ultimately fail, because the social imperative cannot stand without reference to a religious ground. As Karl Rahner observed in his article on "Atheism" in *Sacramentum Mundi,* only a belief in a Creator-God can ground and establish the absoluteness of our moral claims. Secular philosophers from Marx and Mill to Harvard's John Rawls have tried to ground them in humanistic considerations and failed.

Because justice has always been the *bête-noire* of utilitarian theories, contemporary thinkers, following Rawls in *The Theory of Justice,* have revived social-contract theories. For Rawls language about justice enters the world simply because humans are not gross egoists looking for immediate gratification but enlightened egoists intelligent enough to know that respect for others is rewarded in kind. They see that they themselves have a better chance of avoiding pain if they opt for a system in which everyone agrees to sacrifice some of their benefits in favor of the happiness of the group. But when the rules of justice are rooted in such grudging agreements entered into by self-interested parties, justice is experienced no longer as a positive good but only as a necessary evil. As such it stands upon precarious ground.

For the Christian what compels us to act justly and with reverence toward another person is not the Kantian reason that we are all free, or the devices of contracting persons, but the fact of our creaturely dependence. The basic reason why we can say that we all are equal and have a personal dignity is the fact that we are held in existence by a God who has no need of us, but who, out of love, has crafted us from nothing in His own image and likeness. The call to social justice arises not from agreements among self-interested men and women but from the fact of the Creation; it is born not of a contract but of a sense of gratitude.

This has implications for work with the poor and oppressed. While refusing to reduce religion to secular concerns alone, we realize that the so-called secular world is itself profoundly religious. The world is God's creation. It is the only place where we can come into contact with and know God. Even revelation has to be somehow expressed through worldly creation, through words, books, flesh, institutions. If we are created by God, our primary duty is to love God, and our secondary charge is to care for those for whom the Lord cares. Therefore, in a profound way, every social question is itself a struggle between idolatry and the worship of the living God. We cannot completely dissociate spiritual and social questions. We do not get our spiritual energy solely from a spiritual well in order then to go forward to deal with social injustices. No, faith and justice are two sides of the same coin. Though they can be distinguished, they cannot be entirely separated.

And yet there are priorities. There is a delicate balance. Jesus insists that what we do for the poor and the naked and those in prison, we do unto Him; He emphasizes that we meet Him especially among the oppressed. But He also makes a distinction between two closely related commandments. The first commandment is to love God with our whole heart and the second is like unto it, to love our neighbor as ourselves. The two commandments are intimately intertwined but the commandment to love God and be obedient to the Father is first, more fundamental, and grounding. The commandment to love our neighbor is second, less fundamental and in need of grounding.

Of first importance for Jesus, even more than concern for the poor, was a union of love, of affection, of obedience with the Father. Even more essential than the neighbor's material well-being is my (and my neighbor's) personal attachment to our Lord and God.

The poor themselves intuitively recognize this. Though they welcome the aid of the Church in the struggle against corrupt power, they do not want religion reduced into sociology, psychology or politics. I have seen the poor in Brazil walk out of churches when the liturgy took too political a turn. I have known churches in Mexico that have lost two-thirds of their congregation when the social action message became too shrill and drowned out concern about our relation with the transcendent. I have even heard of a Mexican pastor so caught up in political issues, that when he was asked by a woman to administer the sacraments to her dying husband, refused, on the grounds that his efforts for social change did not allow time for such matters. If fundamentalist sects are making headway in Latin America, it is not only because they have strong conservative funding, but because they take time for each individual, welcome each person, place our personal relation to the transcendent at the very center of religion and passionately sing about it.

Though they crave relief for their plight and the help of the Church in obtaining it, the poor of the third world do not want religion to be totally transmuted into a symbolic or a psychological stimulus for political change. Their popular religion is clearly based on a belief in the possibility of a direct contact with God. It is full of intimate conversation with the Lord, Mary and the saints.

Some may object that this is so simply because their consciousness has not yet been raised, that it is a sign that they are in need of "conscientization." But this is too patronizing, and worse, a subtle way of begging the question. If the poor are a privileged place of the Lord's revelation, as liberation theology maintains, then we must listen to them as they are and as God has spoken to them prior to our arrival on the scene. We must listen to how they respond from their poverty. Otherwise we are merely teaching the poor to repeat our arguments and are listening only to ourselves.

It seems to me that in their negative response to a

mere social-action Gospel, the poor are teaching us something. They are insisting that if religion is not primarily an opening unto another dimension that transcends the world, it has lost all meaning; if it is treated only as a stimulus for social concern, it will never generate Tillich's "ultimate concern."

My second point of critique regarding peace and justice efforts as they have developed within Church practice, and more specifically in liberation theology, is that they are too ideological and not sufficiently pragmatic. Most recent discussions of social justice focus almost exclusively on structural analysis and explain it from a Marxian perspective. As a result many peace and justice workers have argued that direct charity does little to relieve human suffering and may actually serve to keep evil structures in place. They insist that such approaches must be superseded by one that emphasizes social analysis and structural reform, for this alone will have pervasive and long-lasting effects. In John Grindel's words: "The great contribution of liberation theology has been to recall that throughout history God has freed people not only from personal sin but also from those institutions that restrain and enslave the human person."[4]

So insistent are some on purging the Church of works of direct charity and personal love that they have criticized the efforts of Mother Teresa. They ask whether it is better to give the poor a fish or a fishing rod. She is undisturbed and gently responds that both are necessary, but that love is more important to the poor than even bread. She says that she will give the poor a fish and that when they are stronger they may also be able to use the fishing rod provided by others.

It must also be remembered that to be done adequately structural social analysis takes great expertise. Even the American bishops' decrees on the economy have been respectfully criticized for not taking sufficient cognizance of sophisticated developments in economics in the last twenty years. Their call for full employment

[4] "The Church in the United States as Prophet," *Religious Life at the Crossroads,* Paulist Press, 1985, p. 99.

without inflation has been declared impracticable even by very sympathetic economists. This does not imply that we should leave economic matters to secularistic technocrats or that we should not engage the poor themselves in an analysis of their situations. On the contrary, I believe the Church and religious congregations should take economics even more seriously than they do. First, the effort should not be strangled by passionate and fundamentalist adherence to outmoded ideologies. And secondly, Church leaders, religious superiors and others, should find ways of collaborating on these issues. They should coordinate their efforts and release a significant number of their most capable members for advanced training, academic and experiential, in disciplines that wed economics and theology.

We now know that contemporary world economics is resistant to analysis in terms of a rigid ideology such as Marxism or scientific socialism. This has been proven with a vengeance by the collapse of Marxism in Russia, its arch-protagonist. Slavish adherence to ideologies blinds us to differences and to a host of feasible options. It tends to stifle the imagination and become weighed down with the heavy jargon of a non-imaginative scholasticism. It is interesting that the recent revolt of the Indians of Chiapas, in Mexico, holds a power of attraction for all Mexicans precisely because it does not use the language of scientific socialism. Middle class supporters of their revolution have said: "These people do not use the abstract language of the left. They express themselves with such inspirational poetry." It was as if someone had released the Indian soul of Mexico, so long oppressed, and all saw that it was beautiful.

When I criticize ideology I am not limiting myself to the Marxist one. We must be careful, too, not to allow the Church's effort in social justice to be automatically defined by liberal politics. In saying this I am not automatically arguing for a full-blown conservative politics, but for a social doctrine that does not become locked in doctrinaire considerations of any kind. We must remain sensitive to the fine grain of each situation, be open to other possible explanations, and be ready to modify our approaches based on experience. Take the population issue as an example. For many years now left-style thinkers, following Paul Ehrlich, have revived the theories of Malthus in arguing for population control. They accept as irrefragable the assumptions of Malthus that the number of people coming to the table of humanity is potentially infinite while the resources of the table are finite. Of course, if this were true, the only option available for feeding everyone would be to cut down the number coming to table. However, in his book *The Ultimate Resource*, Julian Simon contends that a study of history reveals the error of Malthus' central claim: that the resources are finite. By means of a convincing historical analysis, Simon shows that the quantity of any particular resource has increased either in itself or in some humanly devised substitute. On the short term a shortage of a particular resource can occur. But this only stimulates human ingenuity, inventiveness and outlays of money, and before long the problem is solved. The oil crisis of the 1970's is a case in point. There was a brief period of shortage, which prompted worldwide efforts to develop alternative sources of energy, from nuclear fuel, synthetic fuels, to the use of wind and the tides. The world is now awash in oil and the worry is that its price is too low. A similar analysis will show that the ghosts of famine unleashed by the so-called Club of Rome in the late 1960's were laid by the "green revolution." Today even India with its gigantic hordes is a net exporter of wheat.

On this theory, the ultimate resource, then, is the human brain, whose pragmatism is able to transform the quantity of our resources from finite to indefinite and near-infinite. Simon's retort to Malthus is not only stimulating and fresh compared with those of the gloom-and-doomers on the left, but it has the significant merit of being supported by history. It relativizes the Malthusian proposition, periodically resuscitated, that the numbers at table be reduced lest they find nothing there to eat. It is not sufficient that we in the Church approach the problems of the poor with great passion, but that we also approach them intelligently and free of ideological blinders, so that the ends we select be worthy and the means we espouse be effective.

I have the sense, however, that the liberationist and structuralist trend among the Jesuits and the Church in general is on the wane. This is only partly due to the demise of scientific socialism around the world and with it the demotion of its form of structural analysis. It is due also to the recognition that two of the creators of Paul Ricoeur's famous "hermeneutics of suspicion," Marx and Freud, are receding as influences in American culture, and that the third, Nietzsche, is in the ascendancy. His influence is seen in the blatant skepticism of an academic and popular deconstructionism. Nietzsche's critique is aimed precisely at first world Western culture and its value underpinnings. He called for a dismantling of all of its Christian values as inhibitory of the freedom and creativity of the individual. He questions our very ability to attain stable truth of any kind. He declared a cultural war, and it is in such a war that we are now engaged in our post-modern American world.

There is a subtle shift in religious communities toward a re-embracing of the contemplative dimension and a new interest in elements of asceticism, spiritual direction and common prayer. There is resistance too, to the style of recent peace and justice efforts. We are beginning to recognize, I believe, that on one point Nietzsche was right — the motor of history is not economics or social structures but values and culture. The texture of society is not ruled so much by the economic or social structures we have created as by the freely chosen values that are embedded in those structures. On this view, as vehicles of change, economic factors are important but remain secondary. As the 1994 Carnegie Corporation report on children reveals, the well-being of children actually worsened during a period when government spending for them increased and poverty was on the decline.

Even more important than economics is the state of religious belief in a society and the proper understanding of freedom and tolerance. Most disturbing is an understanding of freedom which demands that people compartmentalize their lives. In the first world people tend to separate their public careers from their private lives, and even to re-segment their private lives into separate areas: recreation, time with children, morality, and then religion. Religion increasingly becomes a private affair, bereft of communal aspects, and is often not even related to a church. In this way society has set the stage for a kind of tolerance that goes way beyond respect for others, and is fearful of declaring any opinion to be true or false.

In light of this agnostic quality of modern society, academically labelled a "deconstructionist" society, the question of relevance must again be raised. What does it really mean for members of religious congregations to be relevant today? Is the effort for peace and justice the only mode of relevance? Perhaps not many make such an absolute claim. But is it even the primary mode of relevance for the Church and religious in the 1990's? Are there not more insidious devils to be caught and tamed — a secularization turning into secularism, a cult of arbitrary freedom in which the objective character of morals is questioned, a cultural crusade being waged in the first world under the banner of "political correctness"? Can it not be asked whether the Jesuits and many other religious congregations, have not been somewhat short-sighted in their all-encompassing shift to a faith that does justice? May they have not de-emphasized formal education at a time when the first world is seeking a new apologetics, a kind of "remedial Catholicism," which goes beyond questions of meaning and which provides deep responses to questions about the truth of Christian revelation and about faith and morals? All this is in response to the complaints being voiced ever more loudly in Catholic educational circles concerning the "religious illiteracy" of young Catholics. In other words, in a time of deep de-Christianization, have the Jesuits with their 28 United States colleges and universities and double the number of high schools, and other religious congregations dedicated to education, erred in some measure in their global apostolic planning? Have they and other religious retreated from the field of education and diminished the Catholic nature of their schools and universities at the very time when a strengthening was needed? When are schools and universities more crucial than when cultural wars rage?

In an article on euthanasia Peter Bernardi, S.J. states that "the Catholic Church is the most effective moral force against the legalized self-killing movement."[5] The words that jump out at us are "a moral force," which could easily be broadened to "a theological force." Despite the dangers of triumphalism, how much we hanker for the days when this was true. It is clear that Dr. Kevorkian and his agnostic cohorts in the media recognize the evangelizing power that a coordinated Catholicism can have. It is no wonder that Kevorkian, referring to Catholicism, warns of a "religious zealotry" that will attempt to impose its narrow religious views on the larger society. In the same way, it is because of fear of the force that a united Catholicism can have that we find an excessive anti-Catholic bias in the media.

In the face of media browbeating, Catholics and members of religious congregations, who have only recently stepped out of the immigrant ghetto, might be tempted by inferiority feelings to beat their breasts and suspect that it is the Church that is wrong. This is understandable, and yet how different from the martyrs of Roman days, how different from the English martyrs, from Thomas More — the man for all seasons — who, if he lived in television times, would be painted as quaint and parochial!

One final and more general point on the topic of social justice that may hit closer to home to those in religious life: A few years ago I was at a meeting of

[5] "Coming Soon: Your Neighborhood T.S.C." *America*, April 30, 1994, p. 8.

religious superiors at which the primary topic was injustice toward women in the Church and the lack of empowerment of the laity. After a morning of exchanging ideas and venting anger, at Mass we were confronted by the text from Luke 22:27 where Jesus asked: "And who is greater, he who sits at table or he who serves?" and Jesus answered: "Of course, he who sits at table." But then Jesus continued: "And yet I have come among you as one who serves." In the context, the words took on a special force. Jesus' values ran counter to the values of the world. Jesus was a stumbling-block to *all* who sought to sit at table; not only to those who desired to be higher than others, but even to those who were too concerned about *being equal* to others. He said: "I have come among you as one who serves."

The text roused questions that had been smoldering in me for years. More and more I had wondered why we religious were dedicating so much time and energy to the theme of freedom and equality, especially when it had to do only with our own freedom and equality. Why did we project the power-equality schema on every topic of discussion? Why were we insensitive to a host of other theological values present in every issue? Why were we so narrowly focused on worldly power-issues like authority, patriarchy, participative democracy, being black, Hispanic or white, male or female, or simply being "fulfilled"? Why had such matters become so all-consuming? What did they all have to do with Jesus? With being servants? With eschatological realities? With adoration of and union with God? Was this where faith and justice had led?

In the face of this I found myself impulsively wishing that the Church would quickly address what some call its "internal justice" issues, but, paradoxically, not because they were supremely important but because now suddenly they seemed quite unimportant. I simply desired to get them out of the way so that we could concentrate our energies on deeper religious matters.

This is not at all to deny the importance and the

beauty of freedom and of equality. Freedoms of all types are utterly important: psychological freedom to grow, the sense of being valued for oneself, the freedom from stereotype and oppression. Brought up in an Italo-American family, I have some knowledge of how it feels to be stereotyped, to be considered primarily as a member of a group and not on one's personal merits. But I believe that if we have our faith-priorities right we must maintain that though at one level freedom and equality are very important, at a deeper level their significance pales. The goals of Christianity are more profound. There is still the "*unum necessarium*." Judaeo-Christianity cannot be satisfied with the quest for freedom and equality. For, as Martin Buber says, whoever places freedom and equality in first rank "turns aside from true human existence, which means being commissioned and being sent."[6]

[6] *The Eclipse of God,* New York, Harper and Row, 1972, p. 9.

Hegel once wrote: "Religion is about God." It is a sentence startling in its simplicity, upon which we would all do well to meditate. What it reveals is that in the last analysis religion *is not primarily about us.* And when it is about us, it is above all about our union and relationship with God. The balance between faith and justice is very delicate. Faith cannot be reduced to justice; religion cannot become social ethics or politics. In Bishop Butler's words: "Everything is what it is and not another thing." Only when we grasp this will the quest for peace and justice truly flower. Only then will it evolve from a political slogan into a Christian vision.

6. DOGGEDLY RELIGIOUS COMMUNITIES

The discussion of religious community and the form it should take in today's world has been a principal point of focus in the contemporary renewal of religious life. The community issue is intimately linked with the interpretation of authority and how the vow of obedience will be lived out in religious congregations. More than any other aspect of religious life, community living has undergone countless radical developments that call for scrutiny and evaluation.

During the period of experimentation initiated by the decree *Ecclesiae Sanctae II* religious congregations responded eagerly to the Church's call to remove outdated structures and radically questioned all rules and outward observances in favor of fostering deeper interpersonal values. Prior to Vatican II a congregation's formation efforts, both initial and ongoing, were achieved mainly by demanding public and common adherence to structures set down in an ascetical rule that minutely organized the day from dawn to dusk. One's spiritual life, often called the "interior" life, was considered private, something to be disclosed only to God and one's spiritual director. Sharing one's faith publicly and indiscriminately within the community was quite unthinkable.

In the post-conciliar period, however, the conviction grew that because religious life was linked to the mystery of the Church, community life was at its heart and that community must not be a mere formal structure, but an interpersonal sharing that would impact on one's life with God and would witness to society that love and trust are possible. The theological underpinning for this is stressed in *Fraternal Life in Community*, a recent document from the Congregation for Institutes of Consecrated Life. "Religious community," it says, "is a participation in and qualified witness of the mystery of the Church, since it is a living expression . . . of the great Trinitarian "koinonia," in which the Father has willed that men and women have part in the Son and in the Holy Spirit."[1] Religious life viewed as a journeying together toward God has become an important root metaphor for writers on the distinctiveness of religious life.[2] They insist that "what religious have been seeking, whether they realize it or not, and what religious community can offer, is neither surrogate family life, nor friendship, nor the intimacy of small groupings, but faith companionship on the spiritual journey."

Fraternal Life in Community analyzes some of the changes in the Church and society that have jarred community life, the liberation movements that echoed at the meetings of Latin American bishops at Medellin, Puebla and Santo Domingo, the demands for freedom and human rights, the question of advancement of women, the communications explosion, and contemporary consumerism and hedonism. In every instance the document strives to be realistic and to balance positive and negative elements. It acknowledges, for instance, that even if "in some areas the influence of extremist currents of feminism is deeply affecting religious life, almost everywhere women's religious communities are positively seeking forms of common life judged more suitable for a renewed awareness of the identity, dignity and role of women in society, Church, and religious life."[3]

Modern efforts in renewing community life tried to foster real ties in faith and improve interpersonal relationships among community members. Smaller communities were favored over larger, schedules became flexible and tailored to ministries, local superiors (if they existed at all) became coordinators, commands of obedience turned into dialogue, and major superiors were

[1] Boston, St. Paul's Books and Media, 1994 p. 12.

[2] Susan Beaudry and Edwin L. Keel, "Journeying to God Together," *Review for Religious*, May-June 1994, p. 441.

[3] *Fraternal Life in Community*, p. 17.

limited in their power to assign a person to a particular community without its prior consent. More and more the structure as well as the location of a religious community were determined in function of the ministry or ministries of its members. Though it was considered less than ideal, some members were allowed to retain private living quarters near their ministry and join the larger group from time to time to share in peak moments of the community's life. At times, lay persons were invited to share prayer or take up living quarters within the religious community on a quite permanent basis. Community was defined less in terms of living together in one place under a common rule and more in terms of sharing intense moments or quality-time together in prayer or celebration, in dialoguing about the various works of the group and in keeping alive a historical religious tradition.

The new developments came as a relief, especially to female religious whose life under "mother superior" had often been more exacting and suffocating than that of their male counterparts. These new developments continue to be praised as a welcome escape from a patriarchal form of community life erroneously modelled on the family with its distinction between parents and children. Rigid traditional arrangements were blamed for the infantilism, depression and hypochondria manifest in a number of older religious. Members of the renewed communities were considered more mature, competent, autonomous, self-reliant, capable of intimacy, and as more comprehensible to people in the world.

The document *Fraternal Life in Community* notes that while much has been learned and new images have been formed of ideal community life, one of the weak points in the recent period of renewal is the lack of "the ascetic commitment which is necessary and irreplaceable for any liberation capable of transforming a group of people into a Christian fraternity." The 1983 document entitled *Essential Elements of Religious Life* had stated that unless religious build into their lives "a joyful, well-balanced austerity" they would lose "the spiritual freedom necessary for living the counsels." It insisted that "there cannot be a public witness to Christ poor, chaste and obedient without asceticism."[4]

[4] Sacred Congregation of Religious and Secular Institutes, *Essential Elements of Religious Life*, St. Paul Editions, p. 32.

In light of the great effort expended on transforming community life, surprisingly, as we have had occasion to note, renewed communities were not magnets for new candidates. Members departed and vocations quickly diminished, so that congregations that once appeared like "armies in battle array" now seemed pale and frail in comparison. A number of candidates who entered in search of the daily example and edification of their brothers or sisters found the life fragmented and unfulfilling. Somehow, the de-institutionalized communities seemed too ethereal, too trained upon individuals and their growth and fulfillment, and, in their lack of a regimen of recurring community exercises, seemed fit more for angels than for flesh-and-blood humans. The thick sense of the social body was missing.

In some instances, members of such congregations were dismayed by the new developments and banded together with others of similar views and, hiving themselves off from the parent congregation, established reform groups to live out the original spirit through a return to pristine practices. They felt that a radicality had been lost, the desert, the Johannine separation from the values of the world, a deep and literal rootedness in the Gospel. An example of such a reform-group is the new foundation of Capuchins led by Fr. Benedict Groeschel in the Bronx. It was initiated by a number of younger Capuchins who were dissatisfied with current practices. Keen to rediscover the pristine Capuchin spirit and restore structures that were closer to those of an earlier age, they urged Fr. Groeschel and another middle-aged Capuchin to lead them. Referring to the large number of young people who were applying to join this breakaway group, Fr. Groeschel has said: "It is clear that we will have candidates — our problem will be screening and formation." Similarly, a group of Dominican sisters in Toulon, France, have set out to reclaim the primitive spirit of St. Dominic and have returned to a life of study, prayer, mendicant poverty (begging for their subsistence), and personal involvement with the poor. Gathered around them are a number of young men and women whose gentleness and beauty of spirit is transparent.

Comparatively, two out of three of the Dominican provinces of male religious in France — those of Paris and Toulouse — have restored a number of former communal practices including the wearing of the habit and the choral recitation of the office. Unlike the third Dominican province of France, whose spirit remains more critical and whose mores are more "progressive," both of these provinces have enjoyed an increase in vocations and conduct sizable novitiates. One of the Toulouse novices, a young man who relinquished a significant career in the world in order to join, explained that he and other young Frenchmen were attracted to these new reforming Dominicans, because they offered "a consecration that is visible." The priest worker movement in France had adopted an almost invisible approach to ministry, never proselytizing but simply working side by side with the laity in factories and workers' unions. I have heard it referred to as "apostolate by osmosis." Through their implicit and non-triumphal approach, they did succeed in combating and wearing down an inveterate anti-clericalism present in France since the time of the Revolution. But they failed to attract new candidates to their ranks. It was probably due to an excess of virtue. Non-triumphalism is certainly desirable, but if we take too implicit and non-directive an approach to proselytizing and preaching the Gospel, people wonder what Christianity has to offer to the world. We must heed the directive of Peter: "Always be ready to make a defense to anyone . . . for the hope that is in you. . ." (1 Peter 3:15).

A New Form of Religious Life?

As I mention elsewhere in this book, other community developments have taken place in the Church in recent years. Many Catholic lay movements have sprung up, especially in Europe, that have adopted some aspects of religious community life and observance while retaining an essentially secular existence.

Aware of these and other quasi-religious communes, Joseph Holland, speaking in 1984 to the Conference of Major Superiors of Men, predicted that a completely new form of religious life was on the scene. Traditional forms of religious life would survive but in diminished numbers. Holland reviewed the history of religious life and revealed a pattern. Religious life was dominated in turn by different forms, first, the eremetic, second, the monastic, then the mendicant, and finally the Jesuit-style apostolic model of latter centuries. As the newer forms came into existence, they tended to attract larger numbers of candidates while older forms diminished in size. Because the older forms were still valid expressions of consecrated life, they did not vanish entirely but never quite regained their former pre-eminence in vigor or numbers. Thus Benedictine monasticism, that had dominated France prior to the Revolution, survived after it but in far more modest dimensions.

Holland predicted that the next step in the series, the one that would numerically outstrip the Jesuit-style apostolic congregations, would be a hybrid of religious and lay life. More precisely, it would take the form of heightened pockets of spiritual energy within the field of the laity. These religious congregations of the future would retain a lay form in that they would not necessarily take public or private vows (or promises) of poverty, chastity and obedience, and be squarely inserted in the world. Holland's reasons: Vatican II discarded a concept of holiness construed as a contempt for or flight from the world and insisted, rather, that holiness can only be achieved within the world. When these new lay religious movements start to proliferate, predicted Holland, the last form of religious life to dominate the scene, active Jesuit-style congregations, would certainly continue in existence but would not attain earlier rates of numerical growth.

This is a very provocative theory, partly verified in the new Christian lay movements of Europe and Latin America, but I resist it on two counts. First, on the general principle that predictions are very precarious. As English historian Hugh Trevor-Roper insists, the most characteristic feature of history is not its continuity but its surprise. He contends that if historical research has revealed anything, it is that we cannot predict the future by simply extrapolating past trends or extending lines on a graph. Second, Holland's thesis seems to rest on an exaggerated interpretation of Vatican II's interpretation of holiness and the world. Vatican II's notion of Christian holiness, and *a fortiori* its theory of religious life, retains a subtle but salutary notion of "separation from the world" as distinct from an indifference, suspicion or contempt toward that world.[5]

[5] Cf. *Perfectae Caritatis*, No. 5.

I prefer to base strategies for the future on Fr. Hostie's analysis of historical developments in religious life described above (Chapter Three), though even here I remain cautious. Hostie cites examples of older congregations like the Carmelites which experienced resounding growth through a grassroots reform born of pain even at those times when newer congregations were attracting greater numbers.

Historically, says Hostie, real regeneration of flagging congregations occurred not through the efforts of leadership, though these were substantial, but only when a significant group of the members reclaimed the pristine spirit of the founders and began to live it doggedly. Such a reform was hardly ever a mere cult of the past. The most successful reformers were daring and created bold new ventures while cleaving to the deepest insights of the founder.

In present renewal efforts, we, too, have come to the point where the efforts of leaders no longer suffice and a grassroots reform is required. Concerned about diminishing numbers, defections and lack of vocations, high median age, individualism, loss of identity and availability, and eager to foster the retrieval of charisms and development of shared vision, leadership persons have produced beautiful documents and organized renewal programs, charism seminars, communication workshops, visioning groups, faith-sharing groups, etc. They have taken seriously the Church's option for the poor and accepted apostolates and pilot projects that give expression to this option. They have urged a spiritual renewal in the form of directed and thirty day retreats, Clinical Pastoral Education, Myers-Briggs and Enneagram workshops, etc. But despite all these efforts congregations are aging and dwindling, morale is not buoyant, religious leaders are frustrated, and commentators like Gerald Arbuckle speak of a generalized chaos of religious life. David Nygren and Miriam Ukeritis, the authors of the comprehensive attitudinal survey of religious life, consider that we have only a ten year window of opportunity to turn things around.

Does this quasi-ineffectiveness of present leaders' efforts not serve as further proof to the Hostie thesis, that the effective regeneration of religious orders must spring from below? Is not the strong stress placed by the Nygren-Ukeritis report on the need of a visionary leadership from above, hereby somewhat relativized? Must it not be balanced off by an equally strong stress on a leadership from below, arising from religious instincts at the grassroots? The focus placed by Nygren-Ukeritis on the quality of elected leaders reveals a hidden assumption — that the major reason for the crisis is functional, a question of a lack of skills. I do not deny the importance of visionary leadership or of skills, and will discuss them at length in my next chapter, but I believe that it must not blind us to the possibility raised by J.M.R. Tillard, O.P., that the crisis has deeper roots, that it is a crisis of enthusiasm and faith. If this is so, nothing will serve but a conversion of heart in a significant number of members at the base, a re-forming of congregations at the level of their faith.

While I was provincial and vicar-general, I instinctively resisted the implications of the Hostie thesis. I would have liked to believe that the efforts of major superiors in renewal were paramount. I would have hoped that leaders acting from above could effectively foster the formation of reform groups and not have to wait for them to be formed in pain from below. Could not a provincial group together in a community those who yearn to live out more radically the group's charism, inviting them to structure their life as they perceive the founder would have fashioned it today with the new ascetic practices and counter-cultural symbols this might demand? Could not a general chapter mandate that each province set up an experimenting community, one that by trial and error would try to discover the corporate structures necessary to embody and express the founder's charism in today's world? Or is this just too artificial?

A Case-study: The Pristine Marist Community

Let us grant, for a moment, that the source of the reform will be from below, from groups who take matters into their own hands, from local communities. The further question remains for many of us who do not live the monastic life: What precisely would be the features of an authentically reformed community of an apostolic religious congregation? The answer will, of course, differ with each apostolic congregation, but there may be merit in a case-study from which principles may be drawn. I will use the Marist congregation as such a case study — since I know it best — and ask the reader to apply the conclusions to their own congregation.

What would be the essential features of a community that returned to the ideals of the 19th century Marist founder, Fr. Jean-Claude Colin? How would it look? I can quite easily imagine what a return to St. Francis would be like, or to St. Benedict or St. Dominic. But though I am a Marist, I am not quite sure what a return to the spirit of the founder would entail. The pristine Franciscan community would contain mendicants trusting only in the offerings of divine providence, not storing up goods, bank accounts and stocks, possibly not even having medical insurance, living a very frugal life that gives the lie to the consumerist spirit of the day, identifying closely with the poor, helping them to obtain food and even to change social structures, and in all of this offering them friendship and the unbounded joy of St. Francis and the Lord. They would often turn to a prayer of praise of the Lord as a community and personally, and invite the poor to partake in their prayer as well as in their food.

I think I could work out similar patterns for a Dominican community, or one modelled on St. Benedict. But what would constitute a return to a pristine Marist community, a return to the charism of a modern active congregation founded in 1836? What vision, what structures, what lifestyle, what apostolate?

The Marist founder said that the model for the Society of Mary was not some other congregation, not even the Jesuits from which he borrowed much, but only the early Church and its ideal of *cor unum et anima una* (one heart and one mind). Like many founders, he was impressed with the primitive radicality of the early Church and with the quiet presence of Mary among the first disciples. He felt that the early Marists came closest to living out this model after the ravages of the French Revolution when they preached missions in the neglected villages of the Bugey region of France outside of Lyons. They were not attached to any particular institution, but moved from place to place. They preached in a new way, a hidden way, which sought to avoid the stumbling blocks that clerics pose to a person's journey to God: material greed, vanity, pretension and ambition. They went to others in weakness, as men who admitted their own sinfulness. They lived a simple life in residences they did not own, were diligent in prayer, and were buoyed up by the belief that their ministry was a part of "Mary's work" for the Church.

As apostolic religious, Marists fashioned their community life to their work. They had a sense of a job to be done. They felt that they had been called by Mary to carry out a work of mercy to those who felt they were lost and in sin, to those who felt the Church no longer desired them because they had betrayed her during the Revolution. They had to find a way to speak to a very sensitive generation that had just begun to discover its freedom and dignity and tended to reject any institution that symbolized obedience, tradition, or authority. Like most of the founders of 19th century France, the Marist founders were quasi-artists with antennae for sensing the temper of their times. They felt that the world was shifting under their feet and that a totally new approach was required. Modern men and women, so jealous of their freedom, would no longer take dictation. They had to check everything out in experience, and would believe in God not because they were told to do so, but only if they found Him in the restlessness of their hearts.

The questions of the proper interpretation of freedom and the allied question of self-fulfillment are large issues that have been with us since the early 19th century. They exploded in the 1960's and are the central concerns of our culture. What should be the Marist response to these values? What message should go forth today from those who were urged by their founder to be "instruments of divine mercy"? The Marist response to the modern quest for freedom and autonomy is to see it as the contemporary expression of the hunger for God. These values are not something negative to be crushed, but something positive that must be rescued from superficiality.

But if this is at the heart of the Marist spirit, it has several practical repercussions. It means, first of all, that though working with the materially poor is certainly part of the Marist call, it might be so only *indirectly*, something that would not be true for the Franciscans. It would mean that the *primary* focus of a true Marist community might not be faith and justice, as it is for the modern Jesuit, but one of spiritual mediation — to be at the place of meeting between God and the soul, facilitating the encounter by removing obstacles to God's action upon a soul. The Marist vocation might be primarily to the spiritually desolate and abandoned, to marginal Christians, to those confused by a secularized society, to those sincerely unable to believe, to the unchurched who are embarrassed to ask for reconciliation because of the gravity of their sins or simply because they are afraid to say, "Father, it has been *twenty* years since my last confession." I wonder if the ministry of the Marist community is not what it has always been, a ministry to those who are ashamed.

If this is so, a pristine Marist community need not be located, as a Franciscan one almost always must, among the poorest of the poor. It must rather be located in a place, among poor and rich alike, where it will have access to those who fear the Church and are looking for an unobtrusive entry through a back door, or to those who crave the Lord but, for fear of cultural ridicule, are too embarrassed to admit it.

Could it not be a community in the heart of a large city or at the edge of a great university? Should it not be a community that hosts conversations among lay people on things that really matter, on the problems of moral education, of crime and violence, of sexual morality and marriage, on the social doctrine of the Church, on the meaning of faith in a secularized world, a community that acts as a wellspring in the desert of modern loneliness? Might it not even take a cue from the Christian Science Reading Rooms and be found in the heart of a secular city? Could it not be creative and envisage setting up ongoing and floating seminars, e.g., on business ethics, to be hosted once by Merrill Lynch, later by IBM, etc.? Should it not be a community that invites lay people into the overwhelming task of converting our relativistic, multi-tiered culture to the

Gospel? A community whose scope is as deep and as broad as that of *Evangelii Nuntiandi*?

Jesus and Mary as Active in the World

Allow me briefly to continue my case study, realizing always that it is only an example or a thought-experiment that other religious can carry out in reference to their own congregations. As I continue to probe the idea of the pristine Marist community, I see that the widest gulf between us and our founders, between contemporary Marist communities and those of the early Marists, does not reside on the level of the spirit or nature of our apostolic activity. It is located at a deeper level, at what the French call *le point de depart* (departure point) of their life and activity.

Our Marist historians have revealed that the secret core of the early Marists, their departure point, was a profound belief they shared that they had been called together by Mary. They were convinced that Mary *wanted* something of them. Mary wanted them to carry forth her work, the work placed upon her by divine providence of being a support to the Church in these latter days as she had been to the apostles at Pentecost. The glue that bound together the first Marist communities was the lively conviction that Mary was active in the modern world — that she *could* and *did* want something. This was the soul of their fervor. Can we any longer believe that? If we cannot, is it possible for us to go on being Marists? If we simply take Mary as an exemplar, as the first and best disciple, as a model for approaching a secularized culture, as a symbol for a new way of the apostolate — have we not lost the essential point of the faith of our founders?

I am sure that a similar affirmation can be made for most founders of contemporary apostolic religious congregations. For them Jesus and Mary were not primarily models to be imitated. Rather, they are active and they take the initiative. We do not choose them at all — we are chosen. For our founders Jesus and Mary want something and have chosen us to carry it out. Can we believe this again? Can we discover the theological language, the hermeneutic that will re-express it for modern times without losing its bite? I think we can. I think we must, for this is the heart of the matter. This is what filled our founders and their contemporaries with dynamism and passion. For this reason they were men and women driven. In Paul's epistles the Jews looked for signs and the Greeks for wisdom, but our religious charism is not a wisdom, not a body of virtues, not a set of values; it is a call, a vocation, a hounding by God.

If we do not regain this lively sense of God's call, this trust that Jesus and Mary are actively present, all attempts to fashion an authentically renewed community are in vain. According to Lawrence Cada and his associates, the history of religious orders shows that only those congregations survived major transitions wherein the members returned to a deep re-centering and faith in the action of Christ. Real revitalization begins only when two things are accomplished: personal conversion of individuals through a religious experience, and "the coalescence of those members who have experienced a deep change into a network through which that conversion experience is sustained and enhanced."[6]

We must rediscover the obvious — the transcendent in our charisms — and once again interiorize it. This is the transcendent for Marists: Mary wants, Mary calls. What is the transcendent for your congregation? How do your founders express it? How do you stand in relation to this? This, in my mind is the crucial question, beyond which all else is bloodless and pale.

So at the heart of the reform of any religious congregation is a conversion to the primitive faith of the origins. It not sufficient to seek renewal in the simple replacement of the notion of Church with that of the Kingdom in an attempt to widen our apostolate beyond churchy concerns to those of the world. It is not enough to

[6] *Shaping the Coming Age of Religious Life,* N.Y., Seabury, p. 105.

consider a "journeying together" as the basic paradigm for thinking about religious life as opposed to a striving for perfection.[7] This is certainly an improvement on the atomism that has invaded some congregations, and it does insist that the interconnectedness must be based on the sharing of faith experiences. Its major preoccupation seems to remain, however, with the psychological wholeness of the individual and the good interpersonal functioning of the group.

[7] Cf. Beaudry and Keel, "Journeying Together to God," *Review for Religious,* May/June, 1994, pp. 440-451.

Allow me to record here a rather lengthy excerpt of a letter from a New Zealand Marist ministering in Fiji, who is vitally concerned with the refounding of our congregation not in terms of numbers, power and influence, but in terms of "the recovery of its source, its truth, its prophetic power, its authenticity, its heart." He is concerned to decipher what "refounding" should mean and in the process makes certain distinctions.

"Regarding the question of the 'means' and the 'goals' of refounding, I think that this is an essential question to be raised. Is there a 'goal' to a refounding? I would have to say yes. Are there 'means' to a refounding? I am not sure about that at all! There are means for acquiring knowledge, but are there means for acquiring wisdom? I doubt it. I think that 'refounding' is a grace in the full sense of the word, the same grace, in fact, that brought our Society into existence in the first place. I think that *refounding is something offered* to us, something which we receive . . . it is LIFE! or rather it is "a-being-alive"! It is not something that you can seize, plan for, devise. Refounding ought to be an ongoing way-of-being-Marist (or whatever). What is the goal of refounding? The danger of the word 'goal' is that it implies something 'at the end of the line,' something that can be 'worked towards,' and unfortunately even something unattainable. Goals not only have the capacity to invigorate, they can, sadly, also paralyze. And yet I do believe that 'refounding' does have a goal, and that, it seems to me, must have something to do with bringing a particular community to a radical orientation to the Transcendent, which orientation must be the basic determinant of even the concrete lifestyle circumstances of that community, and which enables a truly corporate, loving and ongoing reception of the living 'founding grace,' all in such a way that it constantly informs the corporate consciousness of that community. The transcendent is absolutely of the essence. It is the source, the ground of all that is new, of all that is prophetic and counter-cultural. All this sounds so remote and abstract, even to myself. However, it is something along the lines of what I would say regarding the 'goal' of refounding. I don't see the goal as something 'out there,' something 'lying ahead' of us, or 'yet to come,' or as some clear-cut point of static perfection to be arrived at. I suppose one could say that the goal of refounding is to 'be' in a refounding way."

In its eloquence this quotation reassures me. It brought to mind the entry in Dag Hammarskjold's *Journal*: "It is not we who choose the way, but the way chooses us, and that is why we are faithful to it." In its attempt to grapple with basic issues, it gives me hope, and reaffirms my conviction that what is wrong with many current efforts at renewal is their lack of religious depth. It is depth that we hear tolling in my confrere's letter, the beating of a heart that is deeply in love with Christ and with the mission of the Marian congregation to which the Lord has called him.

My attempt at the retrieval of an authentic Marist community has been a mental exercise in the reform of religious congregations in general. Readers who are members of a different religious institute are invited to repeat the exercise for their own congregation. I am confident they will find in their history similarly vibrant communities based on a vivid and simple faith.

The various forms of consecrated life that have appeared in history can be interpreted as the Spirit's way of giving expression to different existential gestures of Jesus and of recalling different teachings or mysteries. Through its charism each institute underlines some feature of the mystery of Christ, and in so doing becomes a living memory of Jesus in the Church.

In the autumn of 1993, the Union of Superiors General held meetings in Rome to prepare for the Synod on Religious scheduled for autumn of 1994. In a summary of their discussions issued to the delegates, they too, stressed the faith-dimension of religious life. It is presented as a reflection of the original creation by God and a looking forward to the promise of the last day. Chastity, poverty, and obedience are ways of expressing the impatience of the Lord Jesus and of the Church, His spouse, for the arrival of the Kingdom of God. They are aspects of our "eschatological haste." This impatient desire is manifested most poignantly when we enter the desert, the frontier, the margins of the world, and suffer with those who experience the present time as condemnation, death, meaninglessness, illness, or torture. Those who enter the consecrated life renounce those good things of creation that are most often abused, sexuality, money and freedom. The symbolic function of the religious life does not raise it above the life of secular lay persons in any mundane sense of "above." Rather, like Jesus, a religious is content to say: "I have come as one who serves."

Mutual Trust and Collaboration

It is crucial for community that all members of a religious community who are psychologically at the periphery move back to its center and recover a mutual trust in the institute and its members. Once again, a deep faith is essential if such a trust is to be possible. The members of the founding communities of our congregations were able to overlook each other's foibles and put aside personal ambitions because they truly believed that God had called them together. As such they formed "intentional" communities, corporately directed to certain ends, and not merely "associational" ones gathered together in work but making few demands on the individual person.

Trust in one another is an extension of our trust in the Lord's personal call to us and in his activity in our lives. We trust God enough to believe that we are basically in the right place and with the right people. We do not look to another community but try to love those the Lord has set beside us today and see them as primary symbols of God for us. They may at times seem a sorry lot, but they are the ones the Lord has given us; it is with them that we have been called to create a unity and a covenant and to take up a cause.

When we are linked together in trust we do not view ourselves as atomic individuals, but as co-persons, as interdependent and collaborative beings journeying together in a common venture. This means that no matter what work has been parcelled out to us, we do not do it in isolation, fearing that someone may be looking over our shoulder. Rather, we communicate about it with others, request their advice and act upon it. Interdependence means that wherever we are working in a province, no matter how absorbed we are with our own project, we retain a sense of the totality, consider our own the work of the province and express concern for it.

We have not yet discovered the full meaning of collaboration in the Church. By training we are self-sufficient activists hiding from each other through our work. Often religious communities resemble hotels with little shared existence. We are like so many radios tuned to different stations. Collaboration does not mean that we simply work together; it demands a transformation of mind and spirit. It implies a capacity to include others even when we are thinking alone in our own room. It implies the confidence that by including the perspectives and efforts of others, our lives and ministry and even our personal thoughts will be enriched and improved.

To be interdependent we must first be dependent. We must actually believe —not just feign belief — that the other person has something to offer us. Self-sufficiency is not a community builder and often conceals an inner weakness. Real ability is often coupled with humility, the recognition that we do not have to be perfect in ourselves, and that others can fill in for our weaknesses.

Mutual trust means that we do not fear the other person's performance, his or her growth and flourishing or influence over others. Rather, we encourage it — we *give courage* to it. People who trust are not afraid to praise and affirm. To love someone is to wish good things for that person — that he or she will radiate, grow, run, leap and dance. Gerard Manley Hopkins, searching for the salient feature of the life of Jesus, said: "He loved to praise."

Praise, in the form of affirmation, is also an important part of the major superior's task, bringing talent to life through honest encouragement and acclaim, forgetting about remolding personalities and temperaments, concerned only to enlist everyone into the task. His or her goal is to get everyone to contribute and feel that they are co-creators of something important, not by some artful ruse, but because they actually are. The secret of politics is to keep alive in the group the spirit of the beginnings.

We can find many reasons not to trust one another. One is the fact that we have been hurt in the past. How many people complain that they have been labelled in the past, often by someone in leadership, and have never been able to free themselves from that label. They are paralyzed because they feel that they have been cast into a mold in the mind of the group. They fear to break out lest they seem to be acting out of character. Why do we label people and freeze them into a category? "Joe is a social lion," we say. "Jim is an operator and Jack is a naive optimist." Is it because in a secret corner of our mind we feel that if everyone else is of a type, we have more of a chance of standing out as unique and original?

Yes, there are many reasons not to trust one another — we have been hurt in the past. But Jean Vanier, a contemporary saint, offers some advice. He presents several definitions of community life but stresses the following as central: "Community," he says, "is the place of forgiveness." If celebration is the flower of community, forgiveness is its heart. As difficult as it may be, we must learn to forgive and forget. To think we will ever have the ideal community is an illusion. We are all sinful, partly converted and partly unconverted, all blends of lights and shadows. How often should we forgive? 490 times says the Gospel, seventy times seven.

I remember a book by Raissa Maritain with a lovely title, *We Have Been Friends Together.* It retold in detail many of the philosophical conversations among visitors to the Maritains. It is hoped that in the twilight of our lives, as we look about a room and about a province, we may be able to say with fondness, "We have been friends together" — because He called us friends, and we were caught up in His cause.

Doggedly Religious Communities

In his book *Self-Renewal,* John Gardner says that sociologically the most important factor in the renewal of a group is its motivation and self-confidence. "If people are apathetic, defeated in spirit, or unable to imagine a future worth striving for, the game is lost." Besides vision we need grit, courage, and determination. I too am convinced that if we at the grassroots are not determined to turn things around, if we do not stop retreating, if we do not face straight into the world and throw ourselves fully into discerning and living the charism our founder, the future is lost. In the last analysis, it is not numbers that matter. It is never a question simply of numbers. What counts is the quality of our presence, the degree of our commitment, the wholeness of our heart.

The central challenge before us is that as religious we put more completely behind us the divisions and the exaggerated pluralism of the past 30 years and become once again a unified and dynamic force — a force impelled by a dream. This means that we must be wholehearted in our faith and trust, stop looking around and being distracted by our peripheral vision, stop fearing that some grand parade is going to pass us by.

Do not misunderstand me. The fact of pluralism, the different theologies and models of Church are important. They must be discussed and thought through with great learning and expertise. But more important than the intellectual discussions is the position of our heart. Before we can discuss with each other, we must be bound together. Before there can be any unity of mind, a shared vision, there must be one heart, a unity at the affective level. An argument can hope to end in agreement only if there is love between the parties at the beginning and throughout. Otherwise it turns into a debate whose whole meaning is to score points. So I say, discuss, argue, defend different positions, but first make a vow — a vow of stability, so to speak. Decide to stand with the members of this group. Choose to be with them and for them, be loyal to them, make time for them, love them. At Babel they spoke only one language but could not understand; at Pentecost they spoke many languages and could not *but* understand. For at Pentecost the relationship was right — there was *cor unum*, one heart — in the Spirit.

What is needed is to re-forge the *esprit de corps* similar to that present when members of the congregation worked together in formal education in schools, in hospital ministry, or in foreign missions. Then the fact of many collaborating in the same work acted as a principle of unity. In the pluralistic work situation of our own day, unity must be consciously created by concerted effort. We must discover ways of maintaining the sense of a corporate response emanating from one charism.

Our principal challenges are twofold: quantitative growth of our congregations and an enhanced quality of community life and ministry. But these are interconnected and present us with a dilemma. We need strong and worthy candidates to ensure a future, but we will not attract them until the quality of our life together improves in terms of an apparent lively faith, mutual trust and of a sense that we are moving together toward a clearly religious mission.

We need radical people, more and more members who are willing to let go of everything, to forego every wisp of security, even their favorite neurosis, and truly risk; more and more members who do not need an angle, a comfortable corner, a haven, an escape. More who give not as the bourgeois give, comfortably, but who give until it hurts. We need a group of spontaneous rascals who have no fear of the world, who so love the world that they challenge whatever is slick in it by means of a life lived in accord with the Gospel. People who if asked, "Rabbi, where do you live?" as Jesus was, will not hesitate to answer as He did: "Come and see."

Others more conversant with Marist history and spirituality will decide whether in my case study above I have adequately sketched the renewed Marist community. Those of more practical bent might ask legitimate questions about financing, personnel and the like. But one thing is of utter importance: The pristine community of any congregation — if it ever sees the light of day, must not be an exercise *in intellectualizing* about prayer and being conformed to our charism. It must be a community that actually prays, believes, acts and is Jesuit, or Dominican, or Oblate, or Passionist. Its spirituality and vision must not be "generic," but must arise boldly out of its founding charism and be shaped by it. Its members must gain their inspiration from the texts of the founders, know the central ones by heart and store them in their heart. It must be able to challenge the world as well as learn from it. It must be willing to sacrifice its need for ease and be dogged in coming together frequently for community prayer, for community silence,[8] and other common exercises. It cannot surrender to sloth, individualism, and the styles of a consumer society. It must have a backbone. It must be Benedictine, Augustinian, Spiritan, or Carmelite to the core, and doggedly so.

[8] John Main, the Irish contemplative and spiritual director, maintained that what changes us, more than all else, is to sit together in silence before the Lord.

7. VISION AND RELIGIOUS LEADERSHIP

During his four years in office, President Bush often fretted about not being able to satisfy Americans on what he called "the vision thing." The phrase was humorous because if vision is anything, it is not another particular "thing." President Bush was very competent in crises, as he demonstrated in the Gulf War by organizing a grand coalition of allies and achieving a startling victory. On the other hand, he was unable to articulate a comprehensive view of the world and of the needs of America. He seemed to lack a set of core beliefs to which he was viscerally dedicated and that could give contour to his policies. For all of the criticism against Ronald Reagan as the man who presided over a decade of greed, no one accuses him of lacking a vision for the United States in the world.

The Need for Vision in Religious Leaders

As vicar-general of an international congregation for eight years, I frequently heard the complaint that some provincial or district superior, though very competent in managing personnel and finances and in giving each person individual attention, was defective because he simply lacked vision. At times it seemed that it was better to have the wrong vision than to have no vision at all. But what is this "vision thing"? Why does it seem so essential?

The function of vision is to provide orientation, perspective and *esprit de corps*. As an artist establishes perspective by gathering elements of his painting around a center, a person of vision pulls together into a pattern the disparate kaleidoscopic elements of our religious life and ministry. This gives the group an identity, a lever upon the future, a sense that it is moving resolutely toward a goal and is progressively building something. In providing this note of perspective and orientation, this sense of a common project and progress, vision satisfies a basic human need.

"We must create events, not bow down to them," said William Pitt. This means that we must not wait until events encumber us, but go out to meet the future, imagine it, and in some sense shape what happens. It is what psychologists mean when they say we must not be reactive but pro-active. A religious leader with vision does not receive data and information passively, but actively, incorporating it within a projected imaginative schema or general plan of action. In this way he or she provides focus and orientation and turns a random series of elements into a plot and narrative.

We all know how people perk up during a sermon when the preacher abandons ecclesiastical jargon and begins to tell a story. Stories please because they have a beginning, a middle, and an end, and so satisfy our need to give shape to the apparently random events of our life. They link present, past and future and in this way provide us with a sense of being a unified self and a protagonist in some great venture.

The sense of a future engenders hope, and the link with the past provides depth. Anyone who has lived in Rome for a number of years and returns to America experiences the youthful vitality of a country whose culture is still lacking in depth from a historical point of view. This is because, compared to Rome, the United States has no past. There are no stones bearing the imprint of Roman chariots as there are on the *Via Appia Antica*. There is no small pyramid still standing which was seen by St. Paul as he was hurried to his martyrdom like the one near the *Porta San Paolo* in Rome's Aurelian wall. Vision, like history and stories, provides hope and depth, and for this reason it is essential for religious leadership.

But even if we are convinced that strong leadership must be visionary, is one born with it or can everyone in leadership develop it? Is humanity divided into persons who can think broadly and structurally and others whose thinking is hopelessly absorbed in concrete individuals and situations? I believe that the quality of vision can be developed, but that the capacity for vision does vary greatly with each person. President Bush, for all his other admirable qualities, was probably quite devoid of the capacity for vision.

Persons of vision have breadth and scope. They are persons of a vivid imagination. Not satisfied to administer a religious congregation like a mom and pop store, they cast the net widely, and explore all options. They are not stirred by those who argue that something has never been done before, nor by those who are in thrall to the merely novel and the new. The imagination of effective visionary leaders is not only theoretical but practical. Besides being able to envision a future, set a tone, and establish goals and concrete targets, the effective leader is also able to excogitate effective concrete strategies for attaining them and develop structures of community involvement. In this way the visionary is distinguished from the fanatical or the quixotic.

So, another aspect of vision is that it be realistic. This aspect reveals the leader's understanding that in order to be successful a project cannot be iconoclastic but must work within existing and well-established institutions. If any project for the future can hope to be successful, it must take into account, for example, the fact that the most fundamental organization of the Church is that of a series of contiguous dioceses each administered by its own bishop.

This same sense of realism demands that religious leaders have an objective view of their personnel pool, of its weaknesses as well as its strengths, its age, its lack of certain types of training, and that they realize, too, that their personnel pool differs essentially from that of business managers in that as religious leaders they cannot fire anyone. This means that they must develop the skills for dealing with problem people, always kindly but not fearing at times to use confrontational measures, lest they find their time and energy drained by them. In general, realism demands that plans for the future be tailored to the actual talents and possibilities of the group. Possessing vision differs from having a dream.

A Vision for Religious in Parochial Ministry

"I don't just want to fill a hole!" This is a phrase I have often heard on the lips of younger members of male religious congregations the world over. The expression was applied to different realities in different countries, but the fact that it so often recurred was significant. Where, historically, the emphasis of a province had been in education, "filling a hole" meant being stuck for years in a non-administrative post in a school. Where the emphasis of a province had been in parish ministry, the phrase meant being a curate in a traditional parish under a traditional pastor. One might be cynical and interpret it as concealing a desire to be in charge, but I believe it had more to do with craving ministry which was visionary, with being allowed to create a new style of ministry shared collaboratively with the laity. "Filling a hole" meant being caught in a trap of the hierarchical past where principals and pastors made all decisions and others were asked to simply fill in the blanks.

My experience has been that it is mainly younger religious priests, especially in America, who resist parish assignments on the claim that parish ministry is inescapably stultifying, pointing out that, as the parish presently functions, it is virtually impossible to escape the press of administrative and sacramental demands and be freed for the work of evangelization among the unchurched, the marginal and the poor. No matter how much a pastor tries to delegate to lay persons the mundane matters of finance and administration, it is he, in the last analysis, who is responsible for the oversight of the plant. Ministerially, both pastor and curates are totally absorbed by the administration of the sacraments. Weddings are especially burdensome since these demand extra time for marriage instructions, canonical paper work, and wedding practices. Funerals can be disruptive because they occur unannounced, demand attendance at wakes and involve special liturgical preparations. Moreover, a parish priest's time is devoted mainly to saving the saved, spending time with the faithful few who come to every meeting, serve on every committee, and sign up for every workshop. Is the parish really a worthwhile ministry for religious who are called to be prophets and be at the cutting edge of the task of evangelization? In the conventional jargon, does it not entail more maintenance than mission?

At one time I thought that such arguments not only had some merit but were very persuasive. However, the more I reflect on the question of what really is the cutting edge of the American Church, the less persuaded I remain. Given the state of American society — the shredding of the inner-city family through teenage pregnancy and welfare dependency, the spiral of drugs and violence, the religious illiteracy of our youth, etc. — parish ministry may be precisely where the cutting edge of evangelization is located. The great missionary area of the Church is no longer the third world, but the first world of the industrialized West, and the parish is still the principal ecclesiastical unit of that first world. More than any other institution, it is still the place where Catholics gather.

The mission to the third world, with its poverty, heat, impure water and malaria, is physically arduous. It is, however, psychologically more rewarding because of the grateful response of simple people filled with faith. I have seen priests in Senegal force the doors shut in order to stem crowds of parishioners trying to enter overcrowded churches. In the United States, with its hi-tech values and mundane distractions, priests are becoming accustomed to empty pews and skeptical looks. This is due to the fact that the phenomenon of secularization, that had its roots in Judaeo-Christianity, is giving way to secularism, to a neo-paganism and a cultural crisis. This means that hands-on work among people in the first world, though frustrating, is crucial.

It is becoming clear that in the United States we are enmeshed in a cultural war involving the clash of basic values. If the 1960's were a time of social awakening and the birth of many civil rights movements, of blacks, women, and the poor, it was also a time of cultural revolution, of experiments in de-socialization and the radical removal of the restraints of morality and etiquette. Inhibitions of all kinds were banished as repressive. Permanent commitments were shunned. Fornication, divorce, adultery, abortion, and an openness to homosexual behavior became the norm. The use of drugs was rife and even celebrated by gurus like Timothy Leary. Vandalism gave way to random violence and mayhem, and young people refused to yield their subway seat to the elderly. During this final epoch of Romanticism, literature and music became full of anti-heroes and nihilistic images. Irving Babbitt notes that Romanticism "began by asserting the goodness of man and the goodness of nature," and "ended by producing the greatest literature of despair the world has ever seen" (*Rousseau and Romanticism*, p. 209). This can be verified not only from statistics about the inner city but in every family. Each family has a story about how children were well brought up and were lost to the value-influences of the surrounding culture. It is for this reason that religious must not retreat in cavalier fashion from parish ministry and schools but strive rather to energize such ministries and transform them into true missionary endeavors.

The values of the 1960's seem ever more deeply entrenched in contemporary society. The sense of personal responsibility is shuffled off and blamed on economic and sociological factors. Economic determinism has outlasted the fall of Marxism. Must we not work to reinstate the belief that behavior is shaped more by a group's moral value-choices than by economic structures, and that proper values can be instilled through a proper socio-moral education? Must we not teach that a more equitable redistribution of goods, though desirable in some measure, is by itself not the fundamental answer to crime or even to poverty? For example, the gangs that have plagued Los Angeles since the 1960's are not the children of economic factors and racism alone. They are in part the result of bad choices. Though we cannot ignore them, skin color and economics are not as determinant as people think, nor as decisive as cultural self-image and ingrained values. We know this because black people raised in other cultures and who have recently emigrated to the United States have fared differently than African Americans. Haitian and other black-skinned Caribbean immigrants are as upwardly mobile as was any Irish or Italian immigrant.

It is well-known that Koreans have established successful grocery stands and stores in the poorest city slums. They are motivated and disciplined. Their families are tightly-knit units wherein all pitch in to share the burden of work. It is important to find out the reasons for the difference. Clearly part of the reason is that the new immigrants have escaped the soul-destruction wrought by a tradition of abject slavery and the destruction of self-esteem from being raised in a racist culture. But their example also shows that even enduring racist prejudice can be overcome by motivation and the exercise of civic virtues.

In my opinion the prime task of today's Church is the re-conversion of Catholics to the faith and of all of us to a sense of perennial moral and civic values. To everyone, the Church must strive to announce a vision of humankind in which human dignity is not allied solely to personal freedom or choice but more basically to a fidelity and obedience to God and the laws that God has etched upon creation. This means that the primary task incumbent upon religious will be education in many forms, formal and informal. What is evangelization after all but a subset of education? The culture of the first world is still the dominant culture that has a predominant influence on other cultures. It demands primary attention. The process of secularization that has brought Catholics and other Christians to a new maturity of faith, is at the present time in the process of deteriorating into secularism.

There are powerful forces afoot in this society trying to turn things in a direction which attacks the Christian family. Many elements of society are caught up in a binge of freedom that brooks no opposition. They combat not with rational argument but by means of ridicule, skewed statistics and attitude studies displaying what the majority of Americans desire, as if morals were a matter of propaganda or statistics. American philosopher C.L. Stevenson developed a moral theory called "emotivism" which held that morals are rooted in feelings and are a matter of taste. In his principal book he devotes an entire chapter trying to show how his theory does not reduce morality to propaganda. Everyone admits that he failed. Nevertheless emotivism in morals has moved from academia into the marketplace under the name of "political correctness." Its proponents demand that everyone running for public office must subscribe to all the most popular left-leaning causes of the day.

I have often wondered how we can change minds, how we can communicate with such radical unbelievers in a way that does not turn them off. Once when I was teaching medical ethics at Holy Cross in Worcester, I was invited to speak at the University of Massachusetts on the topic of abortion. I prepared very seriously and set down all the arguments against abortion that I could muster. The first question I got was from a woman who asked: "Why is a man talking on this subject?" An answer came to mind: "I could get Phyllis Schlafly to come tomorrow and she would give the same speech. Would it be any more true tomorrow than it is today?" But I just bit my tongue and said nothing. Reflecting on it later, it dawned on me that the truth is not well communicated by logic and arguments. It is best communicated through *beauty*. We must touch not only the mind but also the heart. "The heart has its reasons, that reason does not know," said Pascal. "Deductions have no power of persuasion," said John Henry Newman. "Persons influence us, voices melt us, looks subdue us, deeds inflame us."[1]

[1] *Discussions and Arguments,* London, Longmans Green, 1907, p. 293.

If religious congregations are to be visionary, they can begin by aiming to communicate a vision to the world. They should strive to change the world by setting before it a vision of life more beautiful than the one the world proposes. In this matter I am hopeful. I believe we are coming closer to the time when we will have a hearing. I think we saw the beginnings of it in the homage given to Jacqueline Kennedy on the occasion of her death. Notice what values people praised in her. They spoke of elegance, class, dignity and grace. "She did not seek cheap attention," they said, "she avoided the media, worked hard, and knew that her principal task was to be a good mother, a shepherd to her two children, Caroline and John, sheltering them from the glare of the world." And at Arlington cemetery, next to the grave of her husband, she honored the graves of her two other children, one who lived only two days, and the other who was stillborn at birth. How different from those who are willing to throw the unborn out with the trash. Jacqueline Kennedy was certainly far from perfect. But in comparison to many contemporary leaders she seemed like a saint. The values she embodied were not old-fashioned, but perennial, valid not only for the past but for also for the present and future. "She walks in beauty, like the night," begins a poem by Byron. It is by such quiet embodiments that we will best communicate the Christian message to the world. Where better to foster and feature such models than in the context of a parish, in the nitty-gritty of life, where Catholics gather?

Another argument in favor of retaining schools and parish work in a dramatically transformed fashion is that the Church of the future will be populist. It will be a Church of the people for the people. The Church is being asked to respond to new cultural issues and provide different types of support, psychological and social as well as sacramental, and because of this, priests, sisters and brothers cannot do it alone. In an older Church the priest could readily dispense sacraments that were legally interpreted and encourage people to keep precise rules of Church and morality. But today we are increasingly aware that situations are different and may call for a more nuanced pastoral response. We cannot just begin with a moral principle and apply it to a situation like a mathematical formula. We cannot simply absolve people from sins but must help them form their consciences. In sum, in the modern Church people are in need of a new and complex kind of care, sacramental, social, and psychological.

Priests and other Church leaders acting alone simply cannot provide this type of care. They cannot spend thousands of hours with individuals in psychological or spiritual counselling or be present at meetings of all the support groups. They have neither the time nor the psychic energy. Church members must be trained to take up the responsibility and provide this new type of care for each other. The most zealous among them, whom priests often refer to as "the saved," must be molded into a missionary corps. The parish must become a field of interacting elements throbbing with love and mutual service.

This will be more challenging than it appears. Present parish structures are geared for the needs of an older and passing generation. New structures will have to be developed in the rectory itself, with perhaps several leadership teams doing different tasks. Training for pastoral ministry will have to prepare leaders to shift tracks frequently in an age of rapid change. Parish leaders must be able to assess the talents and weaknesses of the congregation. They themselves must be trained in the science of groups — networking and group dynamics — in order to set up groups of lay people that are able to function on their own. Church leaders in the new populist Church must be facilitators. One of their principal aims must be to extend the numbers and quality of leaders in the Church. They must mold the loyal members of the parish into an outward-looking apostolic corps.

I am convinced that this new Church, the Church as communion, will not be born from its strength but from its weakness. It will come not out of the pockets of satisfaction within the Church but from its wells of pain. It will stem from the marginalized — the marginalized middle class and the marginalized rich as well as the marginalized poor. It will be born of those who suffer the banalization of life in a consumer culture which trades in suicide, abortion, facile divorce, casual sex and the ceaseless chatter of television. It will come from below, from people in pain. Their pain is a place of privilege, the seed, which having fallen into the ground and died will bear much fruit.

The parish will be a privileged locus for generating this new Church. Religious working in parishes must be trained to identify these "leaders of pain" who are present in each parish. They must provide a forum for them to express their needs. In speaking to them, they must avoid ecclesiastical cliches and institutional language and speak in the fresh simple language of the Gospels. They must communicate primarily by listening and assuring people by their attitude that they are aware of their pain and their need for a different type of care. They must urge them to speak without fear of criticism about the reasons for their disaffection with the Church and the world.

Many things will be learned. It will become clear, for instance, that the reason why today's liturgy is often so uninspiring is that it is too wordy, dividing us into speakers and listeners, and that it is bereft of concrete symbols which serve to unite people and knit together the soul. They will see that the liturgical reform of latter years, which in many ways has been a great boon to the Church, must also accept its share of criticism. In its admirable effort to simplify the liturgy and divest it of the heavy accretions of many centuries, has it not gone a bit to the opposite extreme and left us with a liturgy too redolent of the Enlightenment, a liturgy for intellectuals long on words and abstractions and short on mystery, concrete gestures, emotion, human warmth and passion? Is this not one reason why the charismatic movement sprang up so forcibly in the years after Vatican II? Today's sanctuary with its altar facing the people is in danger of becoming a proscenium stage, where eyes are fixed on the actor and the effects of the liturgy are too dependent on his abilities — all this at a time when the world desires a warm participation with God in a theater in the round.

The difficulty of succeeding in a ministry that tries to respond to real cultural needs rises in direct proportion to the increase in the level of people's education. In the past, preaching was just one of the many things a priest did. Today, according to Fr. Paul Philibert, O.P., many people, if they bother to attend at all, expect preaching to be an extraordinary act of instruction, inspiration, and spiritual insight. Yet very few preachers who are limited in their ability show serious interest in doing it better. According to Fr. Philibert they feel locked into an underworld of incompetence and frustration, and many priestly problems with intimacy may stem from their sense of professional frustration.

Because they often have had more extensive academic training, religious priests may be best able to provide good preaching and to play the new and vital role necessary to revitalize the celebration of the Eucharist and of sacraments in general. I am convinced that in recent years the distinction between sacramental and evangelizing ministry has been too sharply drawn. In my experience, the sacraments prayerfully celebrated can be the greatest instruments of evangelization. This has been demonstrated in programs like the RCIA that involve parishioners in the process of accompanying adult converts to baptism as well as in other programs that engage parishioners in a prospective baptism of infants or in ministry to an expectant mother and family. In New Zealand, religious have had great success in organizing support groups for young mothers. A whole field of creativity opens up in the area of sacramental theology and practice.

I no longer believe the objection that funerals and weddings absorb the priest's time and keep him from evangelization of the marginal. Instead, an inspirational ministry exercised at both funerals and weddings can be important means of bringing the Gospel to the marginal. Take weddings. Often those present are young friends of the bride and groom who have not been inside a church for a long time. Whenever I am asked to officiate, I always take pains that the wedding sermon is not only prepared but inspirational, that it deals with the frustrations of relationships as well as with their beauty, and that the whole matter is handled with imagination, poetry, humor and some measure of psychological insight. It has been my happy experience to be sequestered by couples of all ages at the wedding reception for an extended discussion of some personal problem. It assures me that there is a great hunger in the pews for religious themes. The children of secularization are eager to discover a new solidity, a stability of relationship, and the courage to make a commitment for the long-term.

All of this demonstrates that underlying the complaint of many religious about parish work is not some valid point about maintenance vs. mission, but simply a lack of a vision of the challenge that is before us. This is why parish work appears to them like an endless parade of detached events. A proper vision can transform a parish into a missionary base and render work in it extremely rewarding. But vision demands imagination and realism, the ability to image a practical and concrete future. We must discard old patterns which may no longer seem to work and experiment with new ones. Could we not, for instance, have two teams in the same parish, one primarily for sacramental ministry and the other emphasizing outreach? In dialogue with the bishop and the director of ministry of the San Jose diocese, one clerical apostolic congregation attempted a new way of parish involvement. Three of its members formed a community in a rented house and, without taking charge of any parish, provided ministerial outreach to Hispanics in a cluster of three parishes. It was difficult to coordinate commitments and schedules with three pastors, but overall the experiment proved a great success. Sadly, it ended after four years because one person left the team and no other volunteer stepped forward.

Periodic and in-depth evaluations must form part of any attempt to revitalize parish ministry. In order to be valid, such assessments must be systematic and involve the lay people to whom we minister. This is the only way to be objective and is at the same time a way of challenging the laity to assume responsibility for their parish and empower them. I remember how, as provincial, I once invited parents to evaluate one of our high schools. "How does our school rank with the other Catholic schools in the area?" I asked. "You are No. 2," they replied, and explained that a nearby school run by brothers was No. 1 in all respects: in academic excellence, discipline, and even sports. They explained that even if this were not the objective situation, it was certainly the perception in the community. I reported this to the school community and it spurred many improvements. After being consulted, the parents were very interested in the process of change and made important contributions. The dialogue with lay persons, moreover, was refreshing and rewarding.

Vision as Focus

Besides imagination and realism, a third aspect of vision, and perhaps the most important, is focus. Focus is the arranging of particulars around a center and is essential

124

for the setting of priorities and having perspective.

As provincial I made a valiant but failed effort to truly bring a new focus into the apostolic efforts of the province. In my report to the provincial chapter of 1981 I argued in favor of organizing our endeavors around one focus, ministry to the Hispanic and Haitian and other Caribbean immigrants. My argument was that we could not do everything, and that to simply list ten or twenty apostolic directives was too diffusive to energize and point the province in a certain direction.

If it were desirable to choose one focus, I felt it should be one of utmost importance for the American Church of the future, and for this reason chose ministry to immigrants from countries on the southern rim of the United States. I provided statistics: that by 1990 Hispanics would constitute over 50% of the total Catholic population of the United States. All of them were nominally Catholic. Large numbers were being attracted to the Protestant sects, partly out of dissatisfaction with Catholic services. They are often poor, oppressed and subject to prejudice. Ministry among them fit in nicely with traditional Marist apostolates among the French-speaking Canadian immigrants. Because Hispanics and Haitians were all at least nominally Catholic, and they were a young population, there was even hope of future vocations. Young people from among them might well be attracted to a religious group whose primary focus was concern for the poor and oppressed among the Hispanic-Haitian population. The fact that Hispanics have a strong devotion to Mary should endear them to the hearts of Marists.

I noted, furthermore, that among the bishops who had written to me, several, including Cardinal Cooke of New York, had stressed needs in this area. Finally, I assured the chapter members that such a focus did not demand moving out of many of our present parish commitments, since many of them already had a Hispanic-Haitian component. It would simply demand a change of focus.

125

The first objection was: "I can't be involved in such a project, because I don't speak Spanish." My first response to this objection was to point out that if such a focus and vision were adopted, not everyone had to go into a direct Hispanic-Haitian apostolate. One could remain where he was but still make the other a priority to be supported by encouragement or finance. My second response was more important. It was to broaden awareness and point out the many untapped resources possessed by an international congregation. I reminded the speaker that we had a province in Mexico, and that it would be very easy to set up an exchange program. Some of our men could minister in Mexico for a year while some of the Mexican confreres could work in the United States. Many of them had done theological studies in Massachusetts and could already handle English well, while the Mexicans are the most hospitable people in the world and welcome a priest even with halting Spanish. Working in Mexico would also provide our men with a broadening third-world experience. With such a program, we could develop a pool of men proficient in Spanish and make a major contribution to this immigrant population.

But despite my best arguments, the provincial chapter rejected my specific proposal for an apostolic focus for the province. Some argued that it was too narrow in scope, and others that we did not have properly trained personnel. But I was not disappointed. Even if the specific vision had not been accepted, the idea of the importance of vision and focus had been instilled. A seed had been planted, a new approach to the future; fallow ground had been turned over and prepared.

The provincial chapter also taught me the lesson that in a democratic age, members of religious congregations and chapter members do not automatically stand and salute a provincial's suggestions. They must be involved in each process of discovery from the very beginning. The approach must be truly collaborative, one of authentic communication, and in no way a power game. Everyone involved must bring ideas and opinions but also an open mind to the table. Everyone must be assured that decisions have not already been made. Only in this way will there be a meeting of minds that is not only fulfilling for each participant but effective for the future of the congregation.

After the provincial chapter, I adopted far more participative methods at meetings of the provincial council. In the light of our reflections together, we slowly evolved a valuable practical strategy for renewing the apostolates of the congregation. We came to two conclusions: first, that the resistance to the Hispanic-Haitian focus at the chapter arose principally from an understandable sense of fear and insecurity, and secondly, that in our effort to refocus the province's apostolic energies, it would serve no purpose to ask each community to examine their own apostolate in light of the charism of the institute or of the ministerial criteria we had forged over the years. The reason for this was that clearly each community could make a plausible argument in favor of the Marist quality of their particular ministry, and because of inertia and fear of change would certainly do so. So we hit upon the following course: We would not suggest the abandonment of any present apostolate, but instead, in dialogue with several bishops, accept some new apostolates which were in harmony with Marist criteria. Instead of creating conflict by retiring from ministries of long standing, we would stretch our resources, take on the new, and thus inspire hope and, by example, activate change even in our present apostolates. We realized that at some future date when personnel became truly thin, some apostolates would have to be closed, but we were confident that these would not be the newer, more dynamic ones.

In actual fact, the policy worked. Several new apostolates were accepted in line with various bishops' needs, some among the materially poor, specifically, among the Haitians and other Caribbean blacks in Brooklyn, with the Hispanics in Detroit, in a parish and hospital setting in Vermont, and under a subsequent administration in ministry with Native Americans in South Dakota. Since that time, several traditional ministries have been given up and there is a balance of different apostolates in the province. Some of the older apostolates have been invigorated by introducing new ventures in Haitian and AIDS ministry. Why did the policy work? Because it had the three characteristics of vision: imagination, realism, and focus.

Vision as a Goad to Excellence

The provincial who preceded me had mandated an attitudinal survey of the members of the province. It was conducted by a Dr. Lopez, and about 95% of the membership cooperated. The most striking conclusion of Dr. Lopez, often repeated in the province for over 15 years, was: "You are dying, but you are dying happy!" The study had shown not only diminishing growth, but also that the level of contentment in the province was too high. Other groups of the same level of education showed much higher levels of discontent and desire for change. Compared with other groups of men with equivalent education we were just too happy, uncritical, placid, fulfilled, and bovine. The picture he painted was one of a pasture of ruminating bulls.

This phenomenon of non-recognition of crisis, or of a kind of denial, was found to be quite generalized in religious life by the now famous Nygren-Ukeritis study. As it relates to my own province it revealed to me that, as a group of religious, we had not been seekers of excellence, not propelled by a vision. We had been satisfied to muddle through, to lean on our four years of theological studies, to do things family style. It was part of our charm, but it is not sufficient for the present age. Nor is such an attitude in line with the thought of our founder, Fr. Jean-Claude Colin. Talking to the early Marists he had said: "Gentlemen, we must be men of God and be learned too. If you are men of God alone, I tell you, you will achieve nothing." I know that many other founders have spoken to their disciples in a similar vein.

It saddened me to see so low a degree of drive for excellence in my fellow religious, probably based in a lack of trust in one another and a good deal of self-doubt. I was distressed because I knew that with such an attitude we might achieve much as individuals but would not be able to fashion an effective corps. It saddened me because I knew that much more was possible. Teaching side by side with the Jesuits for some 12 years, I knew that, in proportion to size, other religious congregations, including my own, possessed an equal amount of native talent.

The potential was there, but one thing was lacking in the members of our group. They did not aspire. Something was needed — a corporate vision — to stir up the courage to dare, to stimulate the self-trust needed to raise our sights and widen our vistas, to help us think new thoughts and breathe the thin air, to enable us to break out of the ecclesiastical grid that history had placed over the world and see religious life as a life of pilgrims at the vanguard of the Church's effort at holiness and evangelization.

Whatever we do, we must not go with the drift of things and walk leisurely to the grave. We must be confident even in adversity, and not give up joy in the present and hope for the future. But we must also be sure that our sense of well-being in the midst of the crisis of religious life does not result from the psychological mechanism of denial or from a lack of courage or of vision and imagination. We must not go gently into that sweet night. If in the providence of God we are fated to die, let us at least not die happy!

8. RELIGIOUS VOCATIONS: NEW SIGNS OF THE TIMES

In this our final chapter, I will take a second look at the contemporary situation of religious vocations and what it reveals about our times. Some do not think that vocations are an important feature in taking the temperature of a province or congregation. But Sister Patricia Wittberg, sociologist and author on religious life, does not agree. She says: "Whether or not its members acknowledge or are even aware of it, the single most vital issue that any group faces is the retention of its current membership and the recruitment of new ones. Without an assured supply of quality personnel, a group will decline and eventually die."[1] She goes on to say that many religious orders are facing organizational death. She complains that religious congregations have been "accepting their demise rather passively" and have "taken surprisingly few actions to reverse their decline," and quotes Arbuckle and Markham who speak of "a massive denial."[2]

I do not consider the matter of attracting vocations the *most* important feature in analyzing the health of a congregation, but I do believe it is revealing. If few or none in the first world want to join us, especially while they are joining other congregations in significant numbers, this must indicate something. I do not like the argument that the lack of vocations is a blessing in disguise because it forces us to engage and empower the laity. The position of lay people in the Church is not one to be arrived at by default. They should be squarely at the center of

[1] *Creating a Future for Religious Life,* Mahwah, New Jersey, Paulist Press, 1991, p. 82.

[2] *Ibid.,* p. 83.

evangelization even if the seminaries and convents were bulging. Lay people will find their proper place, not through a decline in numbers of religious or by religious becoming more like the laity and vice-versa, but by each finding their proper identity and prospering.

Vocation statistics provided by general houses in Rome in 1993 revealed that of the older apostolic congregations, those alone are beginning to prosper which have missions in Africa, parts of Asia (especially in India and Indonesia), some parts of Central and South America, as well as Poland and Czechoslovakia. The Society of the Divine Word, for instance, mainly on account of vocations from Eastern Europe and parts of the third world, sustained only minimal decline after Vatican II, and two years ago began a statistical upswing. It is now one of the few traditional congregations of male religious to show an increase in numbers over 1965. In general, vocation statistics for the so-called first world remain dismal for all apostolic congregations founded before the 20th century. The same holds true for priestly vocations in most first-world dioceses.

Why are most of us attracting so few vocations in the first world? It is not our fault, you may say, there just are none. It is out of our hands, a question of the culture. The post-industrial world has become secularized, pluralistic and relativistic. Young people are obsessed with freedom, and because of contemporary affluence are offered a rich array of opportunities. Priesthood is no longer a path for social-climbing. Celibacy is more difficult in an open society with few controls on films and media. Recent pedophilia scandals make for a low image of the clergy. Families are smaller than they used to be.

Like you, I have thought of all the good reasons: but all these reasons seem like so many excuses in face of the fact that in Rome one seminary of a religious congregation houses 290 young men who want to be the salt of the earth — young men who have issued from the skeptical, sophisticated, slick, secularized world and the nuclear families of the late 20th century, young men eager to work *quavis mundi plaga* — in any part of the world — to which obedience may send them. Hundreds of others are joining similar congregations in the United States, Italy, France, Mexico and Spain. Large numbers are also entering the many new seminaries called *Redemptoris Mater*, that prepare young men to be ordained for those dioceses that are open to the introduction of the Neo-catechumenate way (*camino*). And in a related phenomenon, thousands are joining Catholic lay movements in Europe and especially in Italy. Most of these groups tend to be traditional in doctrine and austere, if methodically novel, in their formation structures. Is this phenomenon an aberration? Can all these young people be bent on a neurotic search for security?

New Signs of the Times

I believe that the growth of these new congregations and movements is a new sign of the times. As I indicated above (Chapter Three), it is a sign of the times that in the so-called first world a differential has appeared in vocational recruitment statistics. Religious congregations that have progressively de-structured community life and formation programs, have stressed individual autonomy over group-identity, have assimilated religious life more closely to that of the laity, and have lost a clear sense of purpose, are attracting few candidates. On the other hand newer congregations with intense community life and ritualized community structure, new practices of common prayer, and clear community goals are attracting vocations in the hundreds. We may have legitimate criticisms in their regard, in terms of an excessive rigidity, but the question remains: are these groups simply an aberration or do they provide cues for a possible new future?

Here I want to be carefully understood. When I speak of these groups as signs of the times (i.e. as bearers of meaning, as indicators of a possible future), I am *not* urging

133

religious congregations to ape them or to seek vocations from the lay movements that form part of this phenomenon. I believe, rather, that these phenomena provide an *entree* for understanding the heart of today's youth. Why are young people in a secularized society attracted to these groups? Are such congregations and movements, despite evident defects, responding willy-nilly to some of their legitimate needs? We must use every means to understand the young as they really are and avoid projecting our own needs upon them. Only thus might we re-frame our own congregations and modify the direction of our renewal in a way relevant for the 1990's.

Though each of the newer congregations and movements have their own distinctive stamp, they have some things in common. All tend to be quite exacting, traditional in doctrine but innovative in method. Most of them have a strong link with the laity and several have even grown out of a previously founded lay group to which they remain closely attached. They tend to have a rather ritualized *camino* or way, steps or methodology of formation. Their members are bound together by strong ties and nurture this closeness through a set of communal practices or a structured way of life, a rule. Their piety tends to be simple and uncritical. They view the Scriptures primarily as story and play down use of the historico-critical method for fear of fragmenting the Christian message and diluting its impact. Communal reflection and an autobiographical sharing upon reading the Word of God is a primary resource and support for their spiritual life.

I have made an informal study of these new groups by interviewing their founders, directors or members, or through direct participation in their meetings, in an effort to discern their attraction on first world youth. The attraction seems to be threefold. Young people seem to be drawn to groups which are characterized by:

1. Explicit religious goals;

2. An intense community life and community solidarity;
3. A passion for an explicit and worldwide evangelization.

I will discuss each of these attractions separately — mindful, however, that they do overlap.

Explicit Religious Goals

The young are coming to the new congregations and movements in part to fill an inner emptiness, to discover ultimate meaning for their own lives. They come to find a way. In search of a clear and explicit message about the meaning of life, death and resurrection, they are not attracted to a Christianity which has died the death of a thousand definitions. In religious life they are seeking Christian religion as classically understood, not primarily as a way of psychological wholeness or as a spur to social action, but as an answer to human contingency and cosmic loneliness. They speak easily of salvation, of God's will, of holiness, of vocation as a call from God, of the need for community, and are willing to submit to a Spartan rule and an exacting schedule of common prayer. An article on seminaries in the *Atlantic* (December 1990) reveals that much of the same is true for Protestant and Jewish seminarians in the United States. The author says that seminarians at Harvard Divinity School speak about vocation and about being called "with a pre-1960's fervor."

Together with an Italian provincial of an apostolic congregation, I visited the new Neo-catechumenate seminary of Rome and interviewed the vice-rector. He said the Neo-catechumenate's primary attraction for the young was the style of preaching and formation which bore the stamp of the founder, the Spanish artist, Kiko Argüello. I asked whether this preaching was aggressive and fundamentalist, and if so, whether it might not be considered a form of brainwashing. He replied that, to the contrary, the central and oft-repeated message was that of God's infinite love for each person and the great consolation of the living presence of the resurrected Christ in the Church. Essentially a movement for the conversion and training of secularized lay people, the Neo-catechumenate challenges them to become more conscious of Christ's presence and of the concrete responsibilities implied in baptism.

The Italian provincial, himself a long-time member of the Neo-catechumenate, corroborated this. He himself had first been moved by this same message of God's love and the active presence of Christ. Raised as a kind of Italian Pelagian believing that everything depended on his own effort, he now realized that within the Church existed a Power and a Love upon which he could rely. Not freedom, not psychological release, not social action, not even peace and justice, but the explicit religious message that the Lord Jesus is alive and present, was attracting large numbers of first-worlders to the faith and some to the seminary. An evangelical message was moving them.

Two major emphases regarding the communication of the Word are prevalent in today's Church. To avoid the terms "minimalist" and "maximalist," "progressive" and "conservative," I will call them "implicitist" and "explicitist." Implicitists believe that the way to the secular heart is a quiet involvement of Christians in secular humane causes, and so they tend to play down overt talk about Catholic doctrine and Christian themes. Explicitists, on the other hand, quote Paul VI's *Evangelii Nuntiandi* and insist that such a mute involvement is insufficient. Christians must go further and publicly proclaim their belief in the primacy of the Lord and the enduring relevance of the Resurrection. "Without this fundamental clarity," says Andrea D'Auria, one reduces "the Christian fact to something subordinate to the demands, project and contents of the world." It places the Church in a position in which it "absorbs uncritically the surrounding ethico-

[3] Pro Mundi Vita, April 1990, p. 26.

humanitarian values, the content of which has been borrowed from other ideological matrices."[3] Explicitists complain that implicitists are so understated about Christianity, that people wonder whether it makes any difference at all. If you are in love, you cannot help but descant about your beloved.

These two approaches reflect two different faith-stances. Implicitists are Christians who are themselves quite secularized and who embrace modern pluralism. They prefer a Christianity which is not imbibed as part and parcel of growing up in a society, believing that a consciously chosen faith is more vital and personal. They sympathize with the modern conviction that neither nature nor cosmos supplies a ready-made order of meaning, and that we must in part create our own meaning from the various meaning-systems which may be offered. For implicitists such modern ideas are not passing fads but permanent insights. A religion which flies in the face of the new "truths" of pluralism and secularization will be guilty of obscurantism and will have no audience. So it is best that Christians lead people to Christ through a quiet, Tolstoyan dedication to the poor and needy.

Explicitists (constituting most members of the new congregations and movements) are anchored in a different type of faith. They agree that *aggiornamento* must continue and that Christian institutions have lessons to learn from secular critics in terms of assuming responsibility for transforming the world, but insist that the Church must remain always to a degree counter-cultural. The Gospel and not culture must be its primary criterion. They believe that today's pluralism renders the forging of real community difficult and that while a consciously chosen Christianity may be desirable for intellectuals, it cannot nourish the common good of the majority of the faithful. The latter need a clear and explicit framework of doctrines and structures to support their faith in a world where secularization lapses easily into secularism.

For explicitists modern times have been exhilarating,

but also ravaging. Their message is that these times are over. It is no longer 1968 but 1992. The atmosphere is different. There is a hole in the spiritual ozone layer; people *want* the warming trend that this window to heaven presages. They want a clear, direct and classically religious message and are saying to us: "Be either hot or cold."

Intense Community Life and Community Solidarity

A second aspect of the new groups, which attracts the young, is their offer of an intense experience of community and strong mutual support. Young people yearn not only for an explicit religious faith but also for an intense community of faith. I once asked a young member of the lay community of San Egidio in Rome (about which more later), what had drawn her to the community. She said it was their authentic friendship, which she had not found elsewhere. She wondered whence it sprang and soon saw that it was based in the group's rootedness in the Gospel. I asked her what she would do if the person she wanted to marry did not want to be involved. She answered: "The community is my life. It will be a condition for my marriage. I will bring my children with me when I go there to work."

In order to foster this strong sense of community, mutual support and edification, the new groups emphasize celebration, very often the celebration of the Word, and time spent in discussing important religious and apostolic matters. Small things are sometimes given great importance: the type of music employed, the shape and decoration of the altar at Eucharist, a common form of garb, specific reverential gestures at liturgy. Some have devised a way of spirituality, a *camino*, a way of measuring progress in the spiritual life. Others have attempted to restore the community structures and spirit of the great founders. The Brothers of St. Jean in France began as an attempt to rediscover the pristine Dominic.

This desire for a configured community life is in

reaction to an excessive fragmenting of life in contemporary society. It is a form of resistance to what Robert Bellah has called "Lockean individualism" rooted in the "Lockean ideology," which, he insists, has turned out to be stronger than the Marxist one. The English philosopher John Locke conceived of society as resulting from a contract between persons viewed as atoms shorn of all relationships. For Locke there were no limits on the autonomy of persons other than those they freely consent to in entering a quite limited social contract. For Bellah this picture is in direct conflict with the Biblical notion of the covenant. In the covenant, people have a relationship which is prior to the one generated in the social contract. It is the relationship between Creator and created, a relationship which generates obligations to God and neighbor that transcend self-interest, and promises a liberating self-fulfillment through participation in a divinely instituted order.

A sociological explanation of the new attraction to community lies in the banality of life experienced in a nuclear family and in a society with yuppie or consumerist values. Contemporary families do not have many resources of support, no grandparents, uncles and aunts living in for long periods, no cousins hanging around the back rooms. Inserted into a culture which till recently has felt itself self-sufficient and in no need of transcendence as a source of meaning, such families are not able to cope religiously and tend to drift. Because of a failure of nerve on the part of Catholic educational institutions, attendance can even accelerate the loss of faith. As a result, serious young Christians have turned to one another's explicit witness and prayer to shore up their own faith in Christ and God.

But a sense of mutual support cannot occur without common practices, without in some way ritualizing community life. Historian Fr. Jean Coste, S.M. says that in their attempt to refound themselves, religious congregations must avoid three stances: first, the "fundamentalist" solution, which rules out any evolution;

139

second, an emphasis on mere creativity which says: "Our founders created; we will be faithful to them if we too create"; and third, some facile *via media* which distinguishes between practical rules to be discarded, and a spirit or spirituality to be retained. This is because, like flesh and bone, it is impossible to completely dissociate structure and spirit.

Jean Coste does not urge a punctilious return to the founder's rules, but simply reminds us that there can be no spirit without a style, no group *elan* which is not enfleshed in a *corps social*. If we find the original structures and practices unwieldy and dated, we must invent new ones to express and embody our charism and our being together. Community life must be re-ritualized — the founder's values must be given community expression in oft-repeated symbols and practices. Jean Coste knows we cannot return to the degree of control that our founder wanted the group to exercise over the individual, but he queries whether there was "ever a religious group capable of making a real impact on the world without its members accepting that the group monitor their fidelity, for the sake of the values they all recognize as essential?" I believe this question is crucial, and in asking it Coste is in tune with the community concerns of today's youth.

The founders of the new religious movements know it is futile to try to build community by imparting a spirituality only conceptually and leaving it up to each person to live or embody it in his or her own way. All understand the need for symbols and ritual, and at times insist on minute adherence to a stylized set of practices. They understand intuitively that ritual operates at the level of feeling to inculcate important values and to mobilize people. This is because ritual involves also the body, which is the primary self, and brings all the senses into play. Physical acts and sensory experiences engage consciousness with more immediacy than verbalized philosophies or ideas. Through ritual we understand something of our lives and our place in the cosmos and community on a deeper, less verbal, and less cognitive level. "By conforming to models or paradigms that refer to the primordial past and that can be shared by many people, ritual . . . enables each person to transcend the individual self, and thus it can link many people together into enduring and true forms of community."[4]

[4] Evan M. Zuesse, "Ritual," in the *Encyclopedia of Religion*, ed. Mircea Eliade, vol. 12, p. 406.

Passion for Explicit and Worldwide Evangelization

The third aspect of the new groups attracting the young is their passion for evangelization and willingness to minister anywhere on the globe. Two aspects must be noted: first, the stress on an explicit evangelization, and second, the unlimited scope of the commitment.

As we have said, members of these groups are interested in explicit and classical religious themes, so it is natural that they will also prefer a direct and explicitly religious evangelization. They do not recoil from proclaiming that the world will be principally transformed not by time-bound humanisms but by Christians being Church, by their believing that God is in charge of history and that its deepest meaning is revealed in the death and Resurrection of the Lord. They desire to become, in the words of Hauerwas and Willimon, "resident aliens," and "serve the world by showing it something that it is not, namely, a place where God is forming a family out of strangers."[5] In this way the new movements make the Gospel and not modernity their primary criterion. With St. Paul they are convinced that though we must love the earth and its people, we cannot be mesmerized by "the splendor of the world."

[5] *Resident Aliens*, Nashville, Abingdon, 1989, p. 83.

The second aspect of the new movements' passion for evangelization is its worldwide scope, again following the example of St. Paul. To spread an explicit Gospel message, they are willing to face in obedience the precariousness of a life offered for mission in any part of the world. In some groups the members are keen to become itinerant missionaries sent to different parts of the world two by two, and the aspect of "being sent" is an important part of their spirituality.

Living at our general house near Trastevere in Rome, I have had close contact with the now famous lay community of San Egidio. This community began in 1968 during student riots, when a small group of college students came together to read the Gospel and ask what concrete response they could make as Christians. They began with prayerful, tentative steps. Twenty-five years later, in 1993, 2,000 people joined them at Santa Maria in Trastevere to celebrate their silver jubilee. Pope John Paul II came to the celebration and was visibly moved by the Christian zeal of these young people. Numbering over 15,000 members in the world, there are 5,000 in Rome grouped into 200 cells. The movement has three basic pivots: friendship, group celebration of the Word *every* night, and work with the poor. Each member must be engaged in a concrete work for the poor and perform it in an a-political and non-ideological way. They seem to know every gypsy and beggar in Rome, the truly needy and the sham. They run a dining hall (*mensa*) that provides a sit-down meal to 1200 people four days a week — a sit-down rather than a bagged meal in order to preserve the dignity of the poor. They are daring and inventive: working also for the people of El Salvador, Mozambique, South Africa, and Albania. They are enterprising: running a day of peace in a different country each year on the model of the Pope at Assisi. Recently they were the principal negotiators of a peace treaty in Mozambique because they alone had won the trust of the guerrillas. They are ecumenical: Desmond Tutu comes to them; they ask us to provide bed and breakfast for some of their guests at our general house, among whom have been turbaned cigar-smoking Muslims, an Albanian priest imprisoned for over 30 years by the communists, and an Armenian Orthodox bishop from Istanbul.

Most of the other new groups and congregations have a similar passion for world-mission. The Neo-catechumenate movement has sent out individuals and at

142

times whole families as itinerant missionaries into foreign countries throughout Western and Eastern Europe. How do we and our own congregations compare? Is ours a zeal to proclaim the meaning of Christ's Resurrection worldwide? Or are we locked in, corporately, to our own work, our own province, or ideologically, to our own liberation, to a sheerly secular cause? Do we need a change of scope, a new courage to breathe the thin air, a greater solidarity within the whole congregation, a sense of truly Christian adventure which encompasses this world and the next?

Brief Evaluation of the New Phenomena

If my analysis of the attraction of the new movements is correct, how should we evaluate it? Some are disturbed by at least two features in the psychology of the candidates joining the new movements: first, their penchant for an explicit and affective type of piety (called by the French "*intimiste*"), and second, their attraction to a highly structured community which is potentially repressive. The question has arisen: Are the young who join these congregations and movements too self-involved and drawn more to a Jesus contemplating the Father than to a Jesus active among the poor? Are they attracted to tightly-knit communities with a clear religious purpose because they are in need of certitude and security? My answer to both of these questions is yes, the young can, with some accuracy, be described in these ways. But the further question remains: Is their self-involvement and their need for security neurotic or is it legitimate?

Two Taizé monks have told me that large numbers of young people come to sit on the floor to pray and talk with them mainly because they feel abandoned —abandoned by adults too bent on their careers. Recent American and British studies are showing that contrary to an earlier literature, the children of divorced couples *are* damaged, that the damage shows up later and can affect a whole lifetime.[6] More than abandoned, today's young are also

[6] Cf. *Newsweek,* June 8, 1992, p. 20ff. for revealing statistics.

143

moorless because they are brought up in cultures which do not pretend to answer questions about the meaning of life. They are looking for philosophical reference points, for a faith, and for company in faith. They are in greater pain than we know, and in search of an analgesic for themselves.

Young people do not ask in the first instance: "Where is the Gospel being lived?" or "Which group is really doing something important for the poor and the needy?" Unless we recognize that today's youth are individualistic in character and undertrained in matters religious, we are not living in the real world. They are not altruistic enough to immediately query about the needs of others nor religious enough to ask where the Gospel is truly being lived. Knowing so little about religion and Scripture, such questions are beyond them. What they do feel is a painful lack, an emptiness within themselves, and are looking for something to stanch the pain and fill the emptiness. This is why encounter experiences or happenings, like vigils with the Pope in Denver or in St. Peter's square, are so powerful for the young. This is why evangelicals are so effective when they speak to them of being taken over by an experience of Jesus, of handing one's life over completely to a higher power. Today's youths are not evil, but neither are they saints. They are consumers, and tend to be self-involved. Taught to want to have everything, they have tried to do so, and have found it wanting.

People who reject these youthful needs out of hand do not understand how greatly childhoods have changed. Children coming out of these childhoods may need to experience a religion of consolation before they can move to a religion of service. They may need to pass through an individualist period of "myself and God" before they feel secure. They may need strong community support for their whole life. We must not read into them the need of freedom which was the need of our repressed generation. We must take them as they are.

In an earlier day, vocations came from out of a deep

religious sub-culture. Brought up in immigrant ghettoes or in strong Catholic families, young people were brought up surrounded by Christian symbols and practices which served as a support-system for the faith. When the ghetto disappeared and families were weakened by a growing secularism, vocations diminished to nothing. Now, in subconscious reaction to this, lay religious movements have grown up in Europe and even North America to fill the vacuum. These movements are the new structures, the new sub-cultures introducing the young to the faith and sustaining the children of secularization. They provide the place of encounter that young people so crave.

The Paradigm Shift towards Spirituality

And I will go even further. I believe that these movements and this new type of vocation are part of a global shift in modern culture. Rosemary Haughton was aware of it eight years ago when she spoke to a discussion group of professors which used to assemble at the Marist provincial house near Boston College. At the time I could not see it. Today I am a believer.

Even in non-religious quarters there are signs that contemporary Western culture is moving away from a positivistic and individualistic view which fragments ("beyond the liberal model") toward a more holistic view of society and science which can be called "spiritual." Here I use "spirituality" in a neutral sense; it can be either secular (without belief in God) or theistic. I mean that even scholars and scientists, reacting to the atomism and positivism of a science born of Descartes and Galileo, are beginning to view the world as interconnected, as woven into a larger pattern.

This so-called shift toward "spirituality" is evident in New Age groups with their belief in reincarnation and a syncretism of ersatz science and religious exotica. It is evident too in some adherents of the ecology movement who view the earth as a kind of unified organism, sometimes called GAIA, that has powers of regeneration similar to those of our immune system. It shows up in the holistic approach to medicine where the body is no longer viewed as a sack of spare parts but as a "spiritual" as well as a physical unity. It is seen in some forms of feminism that go beyond a mere struggle to share male power and seek rather to redefine success in ways different from masculine success and thus foster new values and new ways of viewing the world. There is a new desire for recollection and contemplation, for sacrality, for contact with God. "The deep divine message in man can be buried and disfigured," says Cardinal Ratzinger, "but it breaks out again and again and creates a path for itself."[7]

[7] *Turning Point for Europe?*, San Francisco, Ignatius Press, 1994, p. 25.

More generally, a cultural critique is emerging which targets both the economic liberalism of the Republicans and the cultural liberalism of the Democrats. It views both currents as extremes that have left us in a quagmire of consumerism and of hyper-individualism. On this view the major cause of both social and economic problems is rooted in cultural flabbiness due mainly to the ridicule to which society has subjected civic virtues such as industry, thrift, sobriety, self-discipline and the deferral of gratification.[8] In the wake of both economic and cultural laissez-faire we have experienced in the words of *Newsweek* "an explosion of child abuse, crime, learning disabilities, welfare dependency, name your pathology." The article goes on to say that the "very strong subtext of the presidential campaign [was] that both indulgences have run their course." There is the nagging sense that "unlimited personal freedom and rampaging materialism yield only greater hungers and lonelier nights."[9]

[8] Cf. Myron Magnet, *The Dream and the Nightmare: The Sixties' Legacy to the Underclass*, N.Y., William Morrow, 1993.

[9] *Newsweek*, June 8, 1992, p. 20.

Mary Ann Glendon of Harvard criticizes current "rights-talk" as a divisive force "unable to deal with the thickening web of interdependence linking persons with each other and with the natural environment." There is a communitarian movement critical of an excessive libertarianism in social philosophy. Its advocates are Glendon and Sandel of Harvard as well as Amitai Etzioni,

Alasdair MacIntyre, Stanley Hauerwas, and David Hollenbach, S.J. This movement is in search of a new definition of freedom not as a boundless and arbitrary autonomy but as an enrichment arising from taking up responsibility for each other in community.

Glendon feels that European legal scholars, though far from perfect, employ a richer view of "rights" derived not from Locke but from Rousseau and Hegel. In French and German law the development of the person is viewed as the "individual's reaching out beyond himself" in relation to others. Rights are positive empowerments and not, as in America, negative freedoms ("to be left alone"). In her view, the sociality that is missing from American rights talk is not to be achieved primarily through government. The "fine texture" of a civil society composed of families, neighborhoods, schools, groups at the work place, labor unions, churches, etc. is as important to the development of personhood as is the political community.

The new Catholic movements and the new seminarians can be understood as part of this larger pattern, this paradigmatic cultural shift. Some young people are already casting off Lockean consciousness. They are joining groups which offer an interconnected view of things and a way to perfection, groups wherein the source of self-worth and inner unity are found in a consciousness of God's love. If God created and cares for me, I am not just a fragment, but a whole person, a protagonist, about whom you can tell a story. If God is real, I am real. I can have a vocation — with Samuel I can say: "Here I am, Lord."

Integration of Consecration and Mission

If I were to put in one phrase why the new groups attract the young, I would say, because these groups stress "being" as much as "doing," consecration as much as mission, faith as much as works. The young favor groups whose life and mission is shaped by a conscious consecration to the Lord in terms of a distinctive spirit and charism.

In a secularized world there is a tension between consecration and mission, a temptation either to retreat into consecration understood in a fundamentalist sense or to slip over consecration and rush into mission. The latter has been the greater temptation in Euro-American religious life, in the sense that most religious applaud intellectually when leadership speaks about being imaginative and innovative, about setting up criteria to discern truly missionary apostolates, or moving from place to place — even if they then don't lift a finger.

There is a temptation, in other words, to define religious life in terms of function. The now belabored distinction between "maintenance" and "mission" does not suffice, because it remains within a concept of religious life seen primarily as function. It urges us to choose one type of function (mission) over another type of function (maintenance). But our problem today is only secondarily the choice of what we do (function). It is more basically one of reclaiming, strongly and inventively, what we are (identity or consecration). We find it difficult to speak of ourselves in terms of a special consecration, because we fear that religious will once again be placed higher than the laity. We prefer to remain with a stance like: "We are all consecrated by our baptism and there is no special consecration in religious life." Consequently, we try to locate the difference between religious and laity in terms of differences in function.

But this is difficult because laity and religious often share the same functions. It trivializes the true meaning of religious life and causes young people to ask: "What difference does it make?" or "Why should I join?" They desire an invitation not only to an adventure but to a concrete *religious* adventure. They are drawn to a life which commits itself to a more literal re-enactment of the life and mystery of Christ. Is it not preferable to say that religious life partakes of the consecration of baptism, is an expression of that same consecration, but an expression of a special type? As religious we live in the Christian dimension, as do all the baptized, but unlike them we also make that Christian dimension our very career; ours is a consecration, a vowing to live the life of Christ in a more literal way, as did the apostles, leaving aside family, sexuality, earning power and worldly career — and re-committing ourselves when we have failed. It is this special consecration built upon baptism that gives our life and mission its special identity and character.

Signs of Hope for the Future

Up till now we have looked analytically at the present. But now let me swing around the world I know and point out signs of hope. In 1965 there were 450 Marists in France. They have now declined to about 160 and have not had a novice in years. The average age is 71. But suddenly at 104 Vaugirard in Paris a vocational discernment community has been set up where reside seven young men interested in a religious vocation. They live a common life, attend school or work, have a spiritual director, take turn cooking meals, share a structured prayer life, have community discussions, etc. One candidate has decided to enter a monastery, another the Marist novitiate. All of them tend to be pious in a pre-sixties sense (*intimiste*) and give some of the 1960's style French Marists the heebie-jeebies. Yet there is a new hope. The French are finally admitting that the religious revival in France is real, and realize that the new congregations and movements have something to say. It is helping them to dare once again to make a direct and explicit invitation to possible candidates to join the Society of Mary.

Something new is at work in Italy. Both the Capuchins and the Marists have decided to receive postulants coming from the Neo-catechumenate movement. Kiko Argüello, founder of the Neo-catechumenate, says he has hundreds of young men waiting to enter religious life, and insists: "They will be trained Christians." The experiment has begun and has not proved easy due to a clash of style and spirituality. There have been at least two positive results: the receiving provinces have been motivated to strengthen the Marist initial formation program, and because of the interface of spiritualities the seminarians have been reflecting on the meaning of a vocation to the particular religious congregation with an intensity I have not seen elsewhere.

In Holland, surprisingly, the Blessed Sacrament congregation is enjoying a significant rebirth of vocations, most coming from the Focolare movement. How have they achieved it? By setting up two communities modelled on the founder's primitive instincts regarding both spirit and structure. In both communities a time was set aside daily for adoration of the Eucharist, viewed by the community as the source of their active care and support for each other. In the first of these communities, a confrere was dying and offered his suffering for vocations. A candidate was accepted as a novice into that community, and he entered into its care for the dying man. The community members met often, to share their joys and difficulties as well as spiritual insights. Two other candidates came and the next year two more, and remained because they found a real community bonded by the Eucharist. The second community took charge of a church in the heart of Amsterdam. Again, an hour of adoration follows the Mass each day. According to the provincial, there are now eight candidates in that community and every week young men drop in asking about religious life, most coming from the Focolare movement. An authentic community, authentic in the sense of being faithful to the origins in both spirit and structure — this is the primary means for presenting a charism and a vocation today.

In both of these experiments, with the Focolarini in Holland and with the Neo-catechumenate in Italy there is a major problem, which Fr. Anthony McSweeney, former Blessed Sacrament superior general, calls "double belonging" or "dual loyalty." Candidates coming from these lay movements have experienced there their first and dramatic awakening to the presence of Christ. It is natural, therefore, that they are attached to the spirit and styles of the original movement. Can the spirit of these groups be grafted to the charism of the receiving community in such a way that this charism constitutes the primary identity? The question is significant and the problem may turn out to be intractable. On the other hand, down the years rich religious charisms have been molded to receive people from many sides of the cultural and spiritual spectrum. It is premature to judge whether the grafting can hold. We must proceed with utmost honesty and transparence; if it is impossible, we must simply admit it.

Whatever the outcome of such experiments, much can be learned from the new groups. From his study of these movements, the Italian Salesian Giorgio Zevini has concluded that religious congregations should re-institute into their formation programs, initial and ongoing, some clear and distinct stages or steps, as attractive and necessary for today's youth. He is hard at work at developing a model of just such a formation program. Fr. Mauro Filippucci, a Marist Assistant General, has explained the power of these movements by the statement: "We have a spirit or charism, but they have a methodology." By this he meant that they stress a set of practices or steps for inculcating a spirit in individuals and in a group, and that in today's amorphous world people crave this. More and more religious are asking themselves how to fashion a methodology for transmitting a charism and spirituality to the heart as well as the head. Beyond merely talking about the founding charism, they want to experience it. They want it to be the centerpiece of their spiritual growth as persons and as a community. Will it profit to import into our formation programs and our communities certain methods used with success by the new groups? Can we adapt the *scrutatio* over the Scriptures from the Neo-catechumenate and other groups? Can we have a monthly celebration of the basic sayings of the founder, where a passage is read, then parallel passages, followed by a period of silent reflection, an autobiographical sharing by some members on what resonance the text has in their lives, ending with a more scholarly presentation by an expert? Do we not need to delineate clear steps or stages of growth together in the spiritual life, set concrete spiritual goals and suggest means for attaining them?

We have talked for a long time of renewal and refoundation of religious life, but is its day now past? Should we not now move to something which it takes courage to utter: a time of *reform*, in the Carmelite sense — re-forming our hearts according to the pristine spirit of our founders, so that we too will be able again to say: "The community is my life"? Must we not reform the congregation, the social body, so that it is not totally de-constructed, de-structured, but remains a *social* religious entity with the ability to energize and edify each of its members and speak with authority and power of Christ to the world? Reforming means returning to the sources, to the beginnings, and examining ourselves in their light, in order to recapture what made the early members a *corps*, an intentional community, an association with a purpose so strong that the group felt free to make demands on the individual. It means re-living the gritty spirituality that characterized the life of our founders, and made their time a sainted time.

We must ask whether in our attempts at *aggiornamento*, with all the good that has been achieved, we have not, with the best intentions in the world, also absorbed a set of "un-Gospel" assumptions which pervade modern Euro-American culture. This much I know from my experience of religious congregations: whenever provinces and formation programs have become overly-politicized or overly-psychologized or where eschatology has been flattened to fit within earthly horizons, they have tended to empty out. (This must be carefully understood. I am here not criticizing sociology, or politics, or psychology as such, but the cultural assumptions they tend to carry.) When in such provinces the authorities have returned to more classical approaches in theology, pastoral ministry and formation, the seminaries have once again filled up. If we are into psychology, it must be a psychology which has Gospel roots. If we are into peace and justice, it must be a religious peace and justice movement. Fr. Herman Wijtten, in charge of peace and justice for the Divine Word Society, has criticized the peace and justice efforts of some religious as remaining too secular and as lacking a religious vision. Avery Dulles, addressing an assembly of Jesuits at Georgetown, said that Jesuits needed "a necessary correction of course" from the direction taken since the decree *Our Mission Today*, of the 32nd Jesuit Congregation, which enunciated the centrality of the theme of faith and justice.

I, too, believe we may need a mid-course correction in the trajectory taken by the renewal of religious life since Vatican II. Young people are telling us that something has gone wrong with some forms of religious life. They are doing it by staying away in droves. Part of their message, I believe, is that religious groups may have taken the religious heart out of things, that the center has not held. Instead, the young are being attracted by people who invite them to love God because God has loved us, and to assume an unashamedly explicit and classical religious identity. They are being drawn to a strong community life which does not shun ritual and common practices. Their vision opens out to worldwide evangelization for which they know they need to be trained and steeled. They desire to belong to a group that tends to its "being" as well as its "doing," its consecration as well as its mission. They want the example and edification of their brothers or sisters. They sense that the failures of priests and religious which fill the news media are not merely individual failures, but also cultural failures, our failure as a group. They do not desire to become part of a suffocating tribe, but neither do they want to be a collection of atoms, lovely marbles loosely contiguous in a box.

We cannot invite the young to join a merely humanistic cause when they are sorely in search of an answer to the meaning of life in the resurrected Jesus. We cannot offer them a life of unconnected individuals when they are hungry for intense community. We cannot introduce them to a group whose spirit is static or overly secular when they are itching to be a scourge upon the world with the counter-culture of the Gospel.

EPILOGUE

At the heart of the religious life is faith, faith understood not intellectually as in reciting a creed, but faith as trust, as confidence, as warm attachment to God. Faith is the experience that God is present in my life and acts in it. Through faith I sense that I have a spiritual life as well as a bodily one, a life which can grow and develop, and whose food is prayer. Through prayer I grow stronger in the conviction that God is there, that He loves me without condition and beckons me, whatever road my life may take, to be as He is. This sense of a spiritual life was especially present during our novitiate — sweet and fiery, yet fleeting — like all first loves. As time passed and we were caught up in the delicious hurly-burly of life, we let things slip. It was only as we grew older, after many falls and risings, that the sense of a faith-filled life came gently back, more quiet now, deeper, firmer, stronger. In some lives, the sense of faith returns abruptly, as if breaking through a fence, like an inspiration that we have been unconsciously blocking. Suddenly God shows through again, like a sun through the morning mist. The return of faith transforms the world and our work, and the way we look at it. It is a token of heaven on earth and of the happy vision of the God of promise. It can make us think that the religious life, for all its difficulties and painful questionings, is more than just worthwhile — that it is in some sense an adventure — and it can be beautiful.